Budge and Toddie, Their Haps and Mishaps

John Habberton, Lucy Gibbons Morse, J. M. Donald, George Routledge and Sons, Woodfall and Kinder

BIBLIOLIFE

BUDGE AND TODDIE

THEIR HAPS AND MISHAPS

AN ILLUSTRATED EDITION OF

OTHER PEOPLE'S CHILDREN

BY THE

AUTHOR OF "HELEN'S BABIES"

THE DESIGNS BY

LUCY G. MORSE

NEW YORK

G. P. PUTNAM'S SONS

182 FIFTH AVENUE

1878

ILLUSTRATIONS

DEDICATION.

THE duty of people to whom books are dedicated, to purchase copies for themselves, was so thoroughly fulfilled by "the parents of the best children in the world," to whom "Helen's Babies" was inscribed, that the author of this book, impelled by the most popular form of selfishness, has sought for a still larger class to which to dedicate his book. He therefore inscribes it to

"EVERYBODY WHO KNOWS HOW TO MANAGE OTHER PEOPLE'S CHILDREN."

laying to his soul the flattering unction that if the compliment is recognized in the usual manner, every man, woman, and child in the United States will buy a copy.

AUTHOR'S PREFACE.

APOLOGETIC AND EXPLANATORY.

WHEN in the course of human events it becomes necessary for a writer to impose five books upon the public within a single year, a decent respect for literary custom demands that he should make known the reasons which impelled him to do so: The author of "Helen's Babies" might evade the subject by admitting, as he is perfectly willing to do, that his books are no part of literature as the word is defined at present. For the selfish purpose, however, of quieting his own apprehensions, he desires to say that, with the exception of this volume, the books he has published since "Helen's Babies" were partially or wholly completed before the story of "Budge" and "Toddie" had gained more than ordinary attention; that they were either under consideration, or were announced by different publishers; and that, as from a sentiment which he took for modesty, and also because he objected to having such hurried sketches appear as the measures of the ability which he hoped in later days to display, he had insisted upon anonymous publication, and supposed that the books would run the brief career of ordinary stories without causing curiosity as to the author's identity. "The Scripture Club of Valley Rest" was to have been published without signature several months ago, but a heavy pressure of other work delayed its completion until lately, so that it appeared but a brief month before the present volume. The immediate publication of "Other People's Children" does not afflict the conscience of the author, for though he would gladly have deferred its issuance indefinitely, the serial publication of the work has created for the complete work a demand for which the public alone is responsible. The author solemnly declares, however, that he has no more manuscripts to inflict upon the publishers and the public, and that if his future literary ventures are not of better quality than those of the past, it will not be for lack of more attention to any single book than has been bestowed upon all his published works combined.

As the characters in "Other People's Children" are the same as those which appeared in "Helen's Babies," and as a certain line of questioning which has been vigorously followed for a year threatens to gain new force, the author begs to assure the public, with the hope that the statement may be accepted as final, that neither book is a recital of his own personal experiences. "Helen's Babies" grew out of an attempt to keep for a single day a record of the doings of a brace of boys of whom the author is half-owner; the remainder of the book came from whatever portion of the human mind is the source of stories generally. Had the author not neglected to change the names of the children, no one of his acquaintances would have declared the book a family history, for even at present a hundred or more worthy couples among his friends insist that Budge and Toddie were drawn from their own children, and that neither the author, nor any one else, can display boys half so bright as their own darlings. As for the adult characters, the author can scarcely remember the time when he was a bachelor, he is positive that he never sold white goods, and that a ten-days' vacation, with only a couple of lively boys for company, is a luxury which he never enjoyed. To the young men who have written to know if Miss Mayton has really disposed of her hand, the author can only say that as the lady never had an abiding place except in his own imagination, her hand will probably remain free forever.

THE AUTHOR OF "HELEN'S BABIES."

NEW YORK, June 25, 1877.

OTHER PEOPLE'S CHILDREN.

CHAPTER I.

THE writer of a certain much-abused book sat at breakfast one morning with his wife, and conversation turned, as it had done many times before, upon a brace of boys who have made much fun for the lovers of trifling stories and a great deal of trouble for their uncle. Mrs. Burton, thanks to that womanly generosity which, like a garment, covers the faults of men who are happily married, was so proud of her husband that she admired even his wretched book; she had made magnificent attempts to defend it at points where it was utterly indefensible; but her critical sense had been frequently offended by her husband's ignorance about the management of children. On the particular morning referred to, this critical sense was extremely active, whether because of unusual surcease from care during the week, or because the tenderloin steak belied its name and was underdone, the author had not sufficient time to determine by logical effort, for he was compelled to devote his entire attention to the art of self-defence. Like a prudent general who acknowledges to himself the superiority of his antagonist's force, he attempted to create diversions, but the weakness of all of these was recognized at sight, and they were treated with merited contempt.

"To realize, Harry," said Mrs. Burton, "how little true personal attention you gave to Budge and Toddie, while pretending to love them with the tenderness peculiar to blood-relationship, is to wonder whether some people do not really expect children to grow as the forest-trees grow, utterly without care or training."

"I spent most of my time," said Mr. Burton, attacking his steak with more energy than was necessary at the breakfast-table of a gentleman whose business hours were easy—"I spent most of my time in saving their parents' property and their own lives from destruction When had I an opportunity to do more?"

A smile of conscious superiority, the honesty of which made it none the less tantalizing, passed lightly over Mrs. Burton's composed features as she replied: "All the while. You misused your time by endeavoring to correct the misapplications of juvenile spirit, whereas you should have so treated the little darlings that wrongly directed energy would have been impossible. An ounce of prevention is worth a pound of cure."

Mr. Burton had always hated proverbs, and now, as he did not know who originated Mrs. Burton's closing quotation, he mentally made a heavy-loaded scapegoat of the wise Solomon, and thought things that should never be whispered in orthodox ears Mrs. Burton continued :

"You should have explained to them the necessity for peace, order, cleanliness, and self-restraint. Do you imagine that, had you done so, their pure little hearts would not have received it all and acted upon it?"

Mr. Burton offered a Yankee reply.

"Do you suppose, my dear," said he, "that the necessity for all these virtues was never brought to their notice? Did you never hear the homely but significant saying that you may lead a horse to water, but you can't make him drink?"

With the promptness born of true intuition, Mrs. Burton went around this verbal obstacle instead of attempting to reduce it.

"You might at least have attempted to teach them something of the inner significance of things," said Mrs. Burton. "Then they would have brought a finer sense to the contemplation of everything about them."

Mr. Burton gazed with admiration almost worshipful at this pure, noble creature, whose impulses led her so irresistibly to the discernment of true motives of action, and with becoming humility he remarked :

"Will you tell me how you would have explained the inner significance of dirt, so that these boys could have been trusted to cross a dry road without creating for themselves a halo which should be more visible than luminous?"

"Don't trifle about serious matters, Harry," said Mrs. Burton, after a hasty but evident search for a reply. "You know that conscience and æsthetic sense lead to correct lives all persons who subject themselves to their influence, and you know that the purest natures are the most susceptible. If men and women, warped and mis-trained as their earlier lives may have been, grow into sweetness and light under right incentives, what may not be done with those of whom it was said, 'Of such is the kingdom of heaven'?"

Mr Burton instinctively bowed his head at his wife's last words; but raised it speedily as the lady uttered an opinion which was probably suggested by the holy sentiment she had just expressed.

"Then you allow them to be so dreadfully irreverent in their conversations about holy things," said she.

"Really, my dear," expostulated the victim, "you must charge up some of these faults to the children's parents. I had nothing to do with the formation of the children's habits, and their peculiar habit of talking about what you call holy things is inherited directly from their parents.

Tom Lawrence says he doesn't believe it was ever intended that mere mention of a man in Holy Writ should be a patent of holiness, and Helen agrees with him."

Mrs. Burton coughed. It is surprising what a multitude of suggestions can be conveyed by a gentle cough. At any rate, the slight laryngeal disturbance to which Mrs. Burton gave expression prepared her husband quite fully for what followed.

"I suppose," said Mrs. Burton, slowly, as if musing aloud, "that inheritance *is* the method by which children obtain many objectionable qualities for which they themselves are blamed, poor little things. I don't know how to sympathize in the least degree with this idea of Tom's and Helen's, for the Maytons, and my mother's family, too, have always been particularly reverent toward sacred things. I know very well that you are right in laying the fault to the parents instead of the children; but I cannot see how they can bear to inflict such habits upon innocent babes, and I must say that I can't see how they can tolerate it in each other; but families *are* different."

Mrs. Burton raised her napkin and with fastidious solicitude brushed a tiny crumb or two from her robe as she finished this remark. Blessed creature! She needed to display *some* human weakness to convince her husband that she was not altogether too good for earth, and this implication of a superiority of origin, the darling idea of every woman but Eve, answered the purpose perfectly Her spouse endured the infliction as good husbands always do in similar cases, though he somewhat hastily passed his coffee-cup for more sugar, and asked, in a tone in which self-restraint was distinctly perceptible:

"What else, my dear?"

Mrs. Burton, suddenly comprehending the situation, instantly left her chair and made that atonement which is always sufficient between husband and wife; then she said:

"Only one thing more, you dear old boy, and even that is a repetition, I suppose. It is this: parents are about as remiss as loving uncles in training their children, instead of merely watching them. The impress of the older and wiser mind should be placed upon the child from the earliest dawn of its intelligence, so that the little one's character shall be determined, instead of being left to chance."

"And the impress is readily made, of course, even by a love-struck uncle on a short vacation?"

"Certainly; even wild animals are often tamed at sight by master-minds."

"But suppose these impressible little beings should have opinions and wishes and intentions of their own?"

"They should be overcome by the adult mind."

"And if they object?"

"That should make no difference," said Mrs. Burton, gaining suddenly an inch or two in stature.

"Do you mean that you would really make them obey you?" asked Mr. Burton, with a gaze as reverent as if the answer were to come from absolute authority.

"Certainly!" replied the lady.

"By Jove!" exclaimed her husband, "what a remarkable coincidence! That is just what I determined upon when I first took charge of those boys. And yet——"

"And yet you failed," said Mrs. Burton. "How I wish I had been in your place!"

"So do I, my dear," said Mr. Burton, "or at least I would wish so if I didn't remember that if you had had charge of those children, instead of me, there wouldn't have happened any of the blessed accidents that helped to make you Mrs. Burton."

The lady smiled graciously and answered:

"I may have the opportunity yet; in fact—it's too bad that I haven't yet learned how to keep anything secret from you—I *have* arranged for just such an experiment. And I'm sure that Helen and Tom, as well as you, will learn that I am right."

"I suppose you will try it while I'm away on my Spring trip among the dealers?" queried Mr. Burton hastily. "Or," he continued, "if not, I know you love me well enough to give me timely notice, so I can make a timely excuse to get away from home. When is it to be?"

Mrs. Burton replied by a look which her husband was

utterly failing to comprehend, when help came to him from an unexpected source. There were successive and violent rings of the door-bell, and as many tremendous pounds, apparently with half a brick, at the back-door.

Then there ensued a violent slamming of doors, a trampling in the hall as of many war-horses, and a high-pitched shout of, "I got in fyst!" and a louder, deeper one of, "So did I!" And then, as Mr. and Mrs. Burton sprang from their chairs, with faces full of apprehension and inquiry, the dining-room door opened, and Budge and Toddie shot in as if propelled from a catapult.

"Hello!" exclaimed Budge, by way of greeting, as Toddie wriggled from his aunt's embrace and seized the tail of the family Skye terrier. "What do you think *now?* We've got a new baby, and Tod and I have come down here to stay for a few days; papa told us to. Don't seem to me you had a very nice breakbux," concluded Budge, after a critical survey of the table.

"And it's only jes' about so long," said Toddie, from whose custody the dog "Terry" had hurriedly removed his tail by the conclusive proceeding of conveying his whole body out of doors—"only jes' *so* long!" repeated Toddie, placing his pudgy hands a few inches apart, and contracting every feature of his countenance, as if to indicate the extreme diminutiveness of the new heir.

Mrs. Burton kissed with more than usual fervor her

nephews and her husband, and inquired as to the sex of the new inhabitant.

"Oh, that's the nicest thing about it," said Budge. "It's a girl. I m tired of such lots of boys—Tod is as bad as a whole lot, you know, when I have to take care of him. Only now we're bothered, 'cause we don't know what to name her Mamma told us to think of the loveliest thing in all the world, so I thought about squash-pie right away; but Tod thought of molasses candy, and then papa said neither of 'em would do for the name of a little girl. I don't see that they're not as good as roses and violets, and all the other things that they name little girls after."

During the delivery by Budge of this information, Toddie had been steadily exclaiming, "I—I—I—I—I—I——!" like a prudent parliamentarian who wants to make sure of recognition by the chair.

In his excitement he failed to realize for some seconds that his brother had concluded, but he finally exclaimed: "An' I—I—I—I—I'm goin' to give her my turtle an' show her how to make mud pies wif currants in 'em."

"Huh!" said Budge, with inexpressible contempt in his tones. "Girls don't like such things. *I'm* going to give her my blue neck-tie, and take her riding in the goat-carriage."

"Well, anyhow," said Toddie, with the air of a man who was wrestling victory from the jaws of defeat, "I'll give her caterpillars ; I know she'll be sure to like them, 'cauzh they'zh got lovely fur jackets, all heavenly green an' red an' brown, like ladies' dwesses."

"And you don't know what lots of prayin' Tod and me had to do to get that baby," said Budge. "My ! It just makes me ache to think about it ! Whole days and weeks and months ! "

"Yesh," said Toddie. "An' Budgie sometimes was goin' to stop, 'cauzh he fought the Lord was too busy to listen to us. But I just told him that the Lord was our biggesht papa, an' just what papas ought to be, an' papa at home was just like papas ought to be, an' *he* always listens to little boys fyst, mamma says. An' the baby comeded. Yes, an' we had to be very good too. Why don't *you* be real good an' pray lots ?—then maybe you'll get a dear, sweet, little baby ?"

The temporary reappearance of the dog Terry put an end to the conversation, for both the boys moved toward him, which movement developed into a lively chase. Being not unacquainted with the boys, and knowing their tender mercies to be much like those of the wicked, Terry sought and found a forest retreat, and the boys came panting back and sat dejectedly upon the well-curb. Mrs. Burton, who stood near the window leaning upon her husband's shoulder, looked tenderly upon them, and murmured :

"The poor little darlings are homesick already. Now is the time for my reign to begin. Boys!"

Both boys looked up at the window. Mrs. Burton gracefully framed a well-posed picture of herself as she leaned upon the sill, and her husband hung admiringly upon her words. "Boys, come in the house and let's have a lovely talk about mamma."

"Don't want to talk about mamma," said Toddie, a suspicion of a snarl modifying his natural tones. "Wantsh the dog."

"But mamma and babies are so much nicer than dogs," pleaded Mrs. Burton, after a withering glance at the husband, who had received Toddie's remark with a titter.

"Well, *I* don't think so," said Budge reflectively. "We can always see mamma and the baby, but Terry we can only see once in a while, and he never wants to see *us*, somehow."

"My dear," said Mr Burton, humbly, "if you care for the experience of another, my advice is that you let those boys come out of their disappointment themselves. They'll do it in their own way in spite of you."

"There are experiences," remarked Mrs. Burton, with chilling dignity, "which are useful only through the realization of their worthlessness. *Any* one can let children alone Darlings, did you ever hear the story of Little Patty Pout?"

"No," growled Budge, in a manner that would have discouraged any one not conscious of having been born to rule.

"Well, Patty Pout was a nice little girl," said Mrs. Burton, "except that she would sulk whenever things did not happen just as she wanted them to do One day she had a stick of candy, and was playing 'lose and find' with it; but she happened once to put it away so carefully that she forgot where it was, so she sat down to sulk, and suddenly there came up a shower and melted that stick of candy, which had been just around the corner all the while."

"Is Terry just around the corner?" asked Toddie, jumping up suddenly, while Budge sullenly scraped the dirt with the toes of his shoes, and said:

"If she'd ate up her candy while she had it, she wouldn't have had any trouble."

Mr. Burton hurried into the back parlor to laugh comfortably, and without visible disrespect, while Mrs. Burton remembered that it was time to ring the cook and chambermaid to breakfast. A moment or two later she returned to the window, but the boys were gone; so was a large stone jar which was one of those family heirlooms which are abhorred by men, but loved more dearly by women than ancestral robes or jewels. Mrs. Burton had that mania for making preserves which posterity has inflicted upon even some of the brightest and best members of the race, and the jar in question had been carefully scalded that morning and set in the sun, preparatory to being filled with raspberry jam.

"Harry," said Mrs. Burton, "won't you just step out and get that jar for me? It must be dry by this time."

Mr. Burton consulted his watch and replied:

"I've barely time to catch the fast train to town, my dear; but the boys won't fail to get back by dinner-time; then you may be able to ascertain the jar's whereabouts."

Mr. Burton hurried out to the front door, and his wife made no less haste in the opposite direction. The boys were invisible, and a careful glance at the adjacent country showed no traces of them. Mrs. Burton called the cook and chambermaid, and the three women took each one a roadway through the lightly-wooded ground near the house. Mrs. Burton soon recognized familiar voices, and following them to their source, she emerged from the wood near the rear of the boys' own home. Going closer, she traced the voices to the Lawrence barn, and she appeared before the door of that structure to see her beloved jar in the middle of the floor, and full of green tomatoes, over which the boys were pouring the contents of bottles labelled "Mexican Mustang Liniment" and "Superior Carriage Varnish" The boys became conscious of the presence of their aunt, and Toddie, with a smile in which confidence blended with the assurance of success attained, said:

"We's makin' pickles for you, 'cause you told us a nice little story. This is just the way mamma makes 'em, only we couldn't make the stuff in the bottles hot."

Mrs. Burton's readiness of expression seemed somehow to fail her, and as she abruptly quitted the spot, with a hand of each nephew in her own, Budge indicated the nature of her feelings by exclaiming:

"Ow! Aunt Alice! don't squeeze my hand so hard!"

"Boys," said Mrs. Burton, "why did you take my jar without permission?"

"What did you say?" asked Budge. "Do you mean what did we take it for?"

"Certainly."

"Why, we wanted to give you a s'prise."

"You certainly succeeded," said Mrs. Burton, without a moment's hesitation.

"You must give *us* s'prises too," said Toddie; "s'prises is lovaly; papa gives us lots hof 'em. Sometimes they're candy, but they're nicest when they're buttanoes" (bananas).

"How would you like to be shut up in a dark room all the morning, to think about the naughty thing you've done?" asked Mrs. Burton.

"We's makin' pickles for you, 'cause you told us a nice little story. This is just the way mamma makes 'em, only we couldn't make the stuff in the bottles hot." (*Page* 14.)

"Huh!" replied Budge, "that wouldn't be no s'prise at all; we can do that *any* time that we do anything bad, and papa and mamma finds out. Why, you forgot to bring your pickles home; I don't think you act very nice about presents and s'prises."

Mrs. Burton did not explain, nor did she spend much time in conversation. When she reached her own door, however, she turned and said:

"Now, boys, you may play anywhere in the yard that you like, but you must not go away or come into the house until I call you, at twelve o'clock. I shall be very busy this morning, and must not be disturbed. Now you will try to be good boys, won't you?"

"*I* will," exclaimed Toddie, turning up an honest little face for a kiss, and dragging his aunt down until he could put his arms about her and give her an affectionate hug. Budge, however, seemed lost in meditation; but the sound of the closing of the door brought him back to earth, and he threw the door open and exclaimed:

"Aunt Alice!"

"What?"

"Come here—I want to ask you something."

"It's your business to come to me, Budge, if you have a favor to ask," said Mrs. Burton, from the parlor.

"Oh! Well, what I want to know is, how *did* the Lord make the first hornet—the very first one that ever was?"

"Just the way he made everything else," replied Mrs. Burton; "just by wanting it done."

"Then did Noah save hornets in the ark?" continued Budge; "'cause I don't see how he kept 'em from stinging his boys and girls, and then getting killed 'emselves."

"You ask me all about it after lunch, Budge," said Mrs Burton, "and I will tell you all I can. Now run and play."

The door closed again, and Mrs. Burton, somewhat confused, but still resolute, seated herself at the piano for practice. She had been playing perhaps ten minutes, when a long-drawn sigh from some one not herself caused her to turn hastily and behold the boy Budge. A stern reproof was all ready, but somehow it never reached the young man. Mrs. Burton afterwards explained her silence by saying that Budge's countenance was so utterly doleful that she was sure his active conscience had realized the impropriety of his affair with the jar, and he had come to confess.

"Aunt Alice," said Budge, "do you know I don't think much of your garden? There ain't a turtle to be found in it from one end to the other, and no nice, grassy place to slide down like there is at our house."

"Can't you understand, little boy," said Mrs. Burton, "that we arranged the house and grounds to suit ourselves, and not little boys that come to see us?"

"Well, I don't think *that* was a very nice thing to do," said Budge. "My papa says we ought to care as much about pleasing other folks as we do for ourselves. *I* didn't want to make you that jar of pickles, but Tod said t'would be nice for you, so I went and did it, instead of asking a man that drove past to give me a ride. That's the way you ought to do about gardens."

"Suppose you run out now," said Mrs. Burton; "I told you not to come in until I called you."

"But you see I came in for my top—I laid it down in the dining-room when I came in, and now it ain't there at all. I'd like to know what you've done with it, and why folks can't let little boys' things alone?"

"See here, Budge," said Mrs. Burton, turning suddenly on the piano-stool, "I think there's a very cross little boy around here somewhere. Suppose *I* were to lose something——"

"'Twas a three-cent top," said Budge, "'twasn't only a something."

"Suppose, then, that I were to lose a top," said Mrs. Burton, "what do you suppose I would do if I wanted it very much?"

"You'd call the girl to find it—that's what I want you to do now," said Budge.

"I shouldn't do anything of the sort," said Mrs. Burton. "Try to think now of what a sensible person ought to do in such a case"

Budge dejectedly traced with his toe one of the figures in the carpet, and seemed buried in thought; suddenly, however, his face brightened, and he looked up shyly and said, with an infinite scale of inflections,

"*I* know."

"I thought you would find out," said Mrs. Burton, with an encouraging kiss and embrace, which Budge terminated quite abruptly.

"One victory to report to my superior officer, the dear old humbug," murmured Mrs. Burton, as she turned again to the keyboard. But before the lady could again put herself *en rapport* with the composer, Budge came flying into the room with a radiant face and the missing top.

"I *told* you I knew what you'd do," said he, "an' I just went and done it. I prayed to the Lord about it. I went up-stairs into a chamber and shut the door, and knelt down an' said, 'Dear Lord, bless everybody, an' don't let me be bad, an' help me to find that top again, an' don't let me have to pray for it as long as I had to pray for that baby, for Christ's sake, Amen.' And then when I came down-stairs there was that top on the register, just where I left it. Say, Aunt Alice, I think breakbux was an awful long while ago; don't you have cakes and oranges to give to little boys?"

"Children should never eat between meals," said Mrs.

Burton, promptly. "It spoils their digestion and makes them cross."

"Then I guess my digestion's spoiled already," said Budge, "for I'm awful cross sometimes, an' you can't spoil a bad egg—that's what Mike says. So I guess I'd better have some cake—I like the kind with raisins an' citron best."

"Only this once," murmured Mrs Burton to herself, as she led the way to the dining-room closet, partly for the purpose of hiding her own face. "And I won't tell Harry about it," she continued, with greater energy. "There's a little piece for Toddie, too," said Mrs. Burton, "and I want you both to remember that I don't want you to come in-doors again until you're called."

Budge disappeared, and his aunt had an hour so peaceful that she began herself to react against it, so she called her nephews into the house. Budge came in hot haste in answer to her call, and volunteered the information that the Burton chicken-coop was a great deal nicer than the one at his own house, for the latter was without means of ingress for small boys. Toddy, however, came with evident reluctance, and stopped *en route* to sit on the grass and gyrate thereon in a very constrained manner.

"What's the matter, Toddie?" asked Mrs. Burton, whose keen eye discerned that the young man was ill at ease.

"Why," said Toddie, "I got into a hen's nesht where there wazh some eggs, an' made believe I was a henny-penny that was goin' to hatch little tsickens, an' some of 'em was goin' to be brown, an' some white, an' some black, an' they was all goin' to be such dear little fuzzy balls, an' they was goin' to sleep in the bed wif me every night, an' I was goin' to give one of the white ones to that dear little baby sister, an' one of 'em to *you*, cause you was sweet, too, an' they was all goin' to have tsickens of their own some day, an' I sitted down in the nest *ever* so soffaly, 'cause I hasn't got fevvers, you know, an' when I gotted up there wasn't nuffin there but a nasty muss. An' I don't feel comfitable."

Mrs. Burton grasped the situation at once, and shouted, "Toddie, sit right down on the grass. Budge, run home and ask Maggie for a clean suit for Toddie. Jane, fill the bath-tub."

"Don't want to sit on the grass," whined Toddie. "I feels bad and I want to be loved."

"Auntie loves you very much, Toddie," said Mrs. Burton, tenderly. "Doesn't that make you happy?"

"No!" exclaimed the young man, with great emphasis, "*that* kind of lovin' don't do no good to little boys with eggy dresses. Wants you to come out an' sit down by me an' love me."

Toddie's eyes said more than his lips, and Mrs. Burton

hurried out to him, prudently throwing a light shawl about her waist. Toddie greeted her with an effusiveness which was touching in more senses than one, as Mrs. Burton's morning robe might have testified to even the most careless eye by the time that Budge returned. Carefully enveloped in a hearth-rug, Toddie was then conveyed to the bath-room, and when he emerged he was so satisfied with the treatment he had received that he remarked :

" Aunt Alice, will you give me a forough baff *every* day if I try to hatch out little tsickens for you ?"

The events of the morning resulted in lunch being an hour late, so that Mrs. Burton was compelled to make considerable haste in preparing herself for a round of calls. She was too self-possessed, however, to forget the possible risks to which her home would be subjected during her absence, so she called her nephews to her, and proceeded to instruct them in the duties and privileges of the afternoon. Her husband, like any other man, and with a man's deplorable blindness to the finer qualities of child-nature, would have considered that the occasion called only for terse threats and rude bribes; but Mrs. Burton was true to her sex and her avowed theories, so she proceeded to appeal to the higher natures of the children.

" Darlings," said she, putting an arm around each boy, "Aunt Alice must be away this afternoon for an hour or two. I wonder who will take care of the house for her ?"

"I wantsh to go wif you," said Toddie, with a kiss.

"I can't take you, dear," said the lady, returning Toddie's salute. "The walk will be too long; but auntie will come back to her dear little Toddie as soon as she can."

"Oh, you're goin' to *walk* to where you're goin', are you?" said Toddie, wriggling from his aunt's arm. "Then I wouldn't go wif you for noffin' in the wyld."

The pressure of Mrs. Burton's arm relaxed considerably, but she did not forget her duty.

"Listen, boys," said she. "Don't you like to see houses neatly and properly arranged, like your mamma's and mine?"

"*I* do," said Budge. "I always think heaven must be that way, with parlors an' pictures an' books an' a piano. Only they don't ever have to sweep in heaven, do they, 'cause there ain't no dirt there But I wonder what the Lord does to make the little angels happy when they want to make dirt-pies, and can't?"

"Aunt Alice will have to explain that to you when she comes back, Budge, but little angels never want to make mud-pies," said Mrs. Burton.

"Why, papa says people's spirits don't change when they die," said Budge; "so how can little boy angels help it?"

Mrs. Burton silently vowed that at a more convenient

season she would deliver a course of systematic theology which should correct her brother-in-law's loose teachings. At present, however, the sun was hurrying toward Asia, and she had made but little progress in securing insurance against accident to household goods.

"You both like nicely arranged rooms," pursued Mrs. Burton, when Toddie demurred.

"*I* don't like 'em," said he, very positively. "They're the kind of places where folks always says 'Don't!' to little boys that wantsh to have nysh times."

"But Toddie," reasoned Mrs. Burton, "the way to have nice times is to learn to enjoy what is nicest. People have been studying how to make homes pretty ever since the world began."

"Adam an' Eve didn't," said Toddie "Lord done it for 'em; an' he let 'em do jusht what they wanted to. I bet little Cain an' Abel had more fun than any uvver little boys that ever was."

"Oh, no, they didn't," said Mrs. Burton, "because they never were in that lovely garden Their parents had to think and plan a great deal to make their home beautiful. Just think, now, how many people have had to plan and contrive before the world got to be as pleasant a place as it is now! When you look at your mamma's parlor and mine, you see what thousands and millions of people have had to work to bring about."

"Gwacious!" exclaimed Toddie, his eyes opening wider and wider, "that's wonnerful!"

"Yes, and every nice person alive is doing the same now," continued Mrs. Burton, greatly encouraged by the impression she had made, "and little boys should try to do the same. Every one should, instead of disturbing what is beautiful, just try to enjoy it, and want to make it better instead of worse. Even little boys should feel that way."

"I'se goin' to lemember that," said Toddie, with a far-away look. "I fink it awful nice for little boys to fink the same finks that big folksh do."

"Dear little boy," said Mrs. Burton, arising, "then you won't let anybody disturb anything in Aunt Alice's house, will you?—you'll take care of everything for her, just as if you were a big man, won't you?"

"Yes, indeedy," said Toddie.

"An' me, too," said Budge.

"You're two manly little fellows, and I shall have to bring you home something real nice," said Mrs. Burton, kissing her nephews good-by. "There!" she whispered to herself, as she passed out of the garden-gate, "I wonder what my lord and master will say of that victory over imperfect natures, of the sense of the fitness of things? He would have left the boys under the care of the servants; *I* am proud of having been able to leave them to themselves."

"I think no room is perfect without flowers," said Budge: "So does papa an' mamma, so we thought we'd s'prise *you*

On her return, two hours later, Mrs. Burton was met at her front-door by two very dirty little boys, with faces full of importance and expectancy.

"We done just what you told us, Aunt Alice," said Toddie. "We didn't touch a fing, an' we fought of every fing we could do to make the world pittier. D'just come see."

With a rather quickened step Mrs. Burton followed her nephews into the back parlor. Furniture, pictures, books, and *bric-à-brac* were exactly as she left them, but some improvements had been designed and partly executed. A bit of wall several feet long, and bare from floor to ceiling, except for a single picture, had long troubled Mrs. Burton's artistic eye, and she now found that tasteful minds, like great ones, think alike.

"I think no room is perfect without flowers," said Budge; "so does papa an' mamma, so we thought we'd s'prise *you* with some."

On the floor, in a heap which was not without tasteful arrangement, was almost a cartload of stones disposed as a "rockery," and on the top thereof, and working through the crevices, was a large quantity of street-dust. From several of the crevices protruded ferns, somewhat wilted, and bearing evidence of having been several times disarranged and dropped upon the dry soil which partly covered their roots. Around the base was twined several yards of Virginia creeper, while from the top sprang a well-branched specimen of the *Datura stramonium* (the common "stinkweed"). The three conservators of the beautiful gazed in silence for a moment, and then Toddie looked up with angelic expression and said :

"Isn't it lovaly?"

"I hope what you brought us is *real* nice," remarked Budge, "for 'twas *awful* hard work to make that rockery. I guess I never was so tired in all my life. Mamma's is on a big box, but we couldn't find any boxes anywhere, an' we couldn't find the girls to ask 'em. That ain't the kind of datura that has the flowers just like pretty vases, but papa says it's more healthy than the tame kind. The ferns look kind o' thirsty, but I could *not* see how to water 'em without wettin' the carpet, so I thought I'd wait till you came home and ask you about it."

There was a sudden rustle of silken robes and two little boys found themselves alone. When, half an hour later, Mr. Burton returned from the city, he found his wife more reticent than he ever had known her to be, while two Milesians, with market baskets, were sifting dust upon his hall-carpets and making a stone-heap in the gutter in front of the house.

CHAPTER II.

On the morning of the second day of Mrs. Burton's experiment, the aunt of Budge and Toddie awoke with more than her usual sense of the responsibility and burden of life. Her husband's description of a charming lot of *bric-à-brac* and pottery, soon to be sold at auction, did not stimulate as much inquiry as such announcements usually did, and Mrs. Burton's cook did not have her usual early morning visit from her watchful mistress. Mrs. Burton was wondering which of her many duties to her nephews should be first attended to; but, as she wondered long without reaching any conclusion, an ever-sympathizing Providence came to her assistance, for the children awoke, and created such a hubbub directly over her head, that she speedily determined that reproof was the first thing in order. Dressing hastily, she went up to the chamber of the innocents, and found the noise was occasioned by a heavy, antique centre-table, which was flying back and forth across the room, the motive power consisting of two pairs of sturdy little arms.

"Hullo! Aunt Alice!" said Budge. "I'm awful glad you came in. The table's a choochoo (locomotive), you know, an' my corner's New York, an' Tod's is Hillcrest, an' he's ticket-agent at one place an' I at the other. But the choochoo hasn't got any engineer, an' we have to push it, an' it isn't fair for ticket-agents to do so much work besides their own. Now, *you* can be engineer—jump on!"

The extempore locomotive was accommodatingly pushed up to Mrs Burton with such force as to seriously disturb her equilibrium, but she managed to remark:

"Do you do this way with your mamma's guest-chamber furniture?"

"No," said Toddie, "'cause why, 'pare-shamber's always lockted. B'sides that, papa once tookted all the wheels off our tables—said tables wazh too restless."

"Little boys," said Mrs. Burton, returning the table to its place with an energy which was somewhat impressive, "should never use things which belong to other people, without asking permission. Nor should they ever use anything, no matter to whom it belongs, in any way but that which it was made to be used in. Now, did either of you ever see a table on a railroad?"

"'Course we did," said Toddie, promptly; "there's a tyne-table (turn-table) at Hillcrest, an' annuvver at Dzersey City—how could choochoos turn around if there wasn't?"

"It's time to dress for breakfast, now," said Mrs. Burton, in some confusion, as she departed.

The children appeared promptly at the table on the ringing of the bell, and brought ravenous appetites with them. Mrs. Burton composed a solemn face, rapped on the table with the handle of the carving-knife, and all heads were bowed while the host and hostess silently returned thanks. When the adults raised their heads they saw that two juvenile faces were still closely hidden in two pairs of small hands. Mrs. Burton reverently nodded at each one to attract her husband's attention, and mentally determined that souls so absorbed in thanksgiving were good ground for better spiritual seed than Tom and Helen Lawrence had ever scattered. Slowly, however, twice ten little fingers separated, and very large eyes peeped inquiringly between them; then Budge suddenly dropped his hands, straightened himself in his chair, and said:

"Why, Uncle Harry! have you been forgettin' again how to ask a blessing?"

And Toddie, looking somewhat complainingly at his uncle, and very hungrily at the steak, remarked:

"Said *my* blessin' 'bout *fifty* times!"

"Once would have been sufficient, Toddie," said Mrs Burton.

"Why didn't you say *yoush* once, then?" asked Toddie.

"I did; we don't need to talk aloud to have the Lord hear us," explained Mrs. Burton.

"'Posin' you don't," said Toddie, "I don't fink it's a very nice way to do, to whisper fings to the Lord. When I whisper anyfing, mamma says, 'Toddie, what's you whisperin' for? You 'shamed of somefing?" Guesh you an' Uncle Harry's bofe 'shamed at the same time."

Mr. Burton was very anxious to give his wife a pertinent hint, yet dared not while two such vigilant pairs of ears were present A happy thought struck him, and he said, in very bad German:

"Is it not time for the reformation to begin?"

And with irreproachable grammar and accent, Mrs. Burton answered:

"It soon will be."

"That's awful funny talk," said Budge. "I wish *I* could talk that way. That's just the way ragged, dirty men talk to my papa sometimes, and then he gives 'em lots of pennies. When was you and Aunt Alice ragged an' dirty so as to learn to talk that way?"

"Budge! Budge!" exclaimed Mrs. Burton, "thousands of very rich and handsome people talk that way—all German people do."

"Do they talk to the Lord so?" asked Budge.

"Certainly," said Mrs. Burton.

"Gracious!" exclaimed the young man. "He must be awful smart to understand them."

Mr. Burton repeated his question in German, but Mrs.

Burton kept silent and looked extremely serious, with a ghost of a frown.

"What are you boys and your auntie going to do with yourselves to-day?" asked Mr. Burton.

"I guess," said Budge, looking out through the window, "it's going to rain, so the best thing will be for Aunt Alice to tell us stories all day long. We never *do* get enough stories."

"Just the thing!" exclaimed Mrs. Burton, her face coming from behind the clouds, and with more than its usual radiance.

"Hazh you got plenty of stories in your tummuk?" asked Toddie, poising his fork in air, regardless of the gravy which trickled down upon his hand from the fragment of meat at the end.

"Dozens of them," said Mrs. Burton. "Only think! I listened to stories in Sunday-school for about ten years, and I've never had anybody to tell them to."

"I don't think much of Sunday-school stories," said Budge, with the air of a man indulging in an unsatisfactory retrospect. "There's always something at the end of 'em that spoils all the good taste of 'em—something about being good little boys."

"Aunt Alice's stories haven't any such endings," said Mr. Burton, with a sneaking desire to commit his wife to a policy of simple amusement. "She knows that little boys want to be good, and she wants to see them happy, too."

"Aunt Alice will tell you only what you will enjoy, Budge, she promises you that," said Mrs. Burton, with the cheerfulness of assured success. "We will send Uncle Harry away right after breakfast, and then you shall have all the stories you want."

"And cake, too?" asked Toddie. "Mamma always gives us cakes when she's telling us stories, so we'll sit still an' not wriggle about."

"No cakes," said Mrs. Burton, kindly but firmly. "Eating between meals spoils the digestion of little boys, and makes them very cross."

"I guess that's what was the matter with the dog Terry yesterday, then," said Budge. He was eating a bone between meals, out in the garden, and when I took hold of his back legs and tried to play that he was a wheelbarrow, he bit me."

Mr. Burton gave the dog Terry a sympathetic pat and a bit of meat, making him stand on his hind legs and beg for the latter, to the great diversion of the children. Then, with an affectionate kiss and a look of tender solicitude, he wished his wife a happy day, and hurried off to the city. Mrs. Burton took the children into the library, and picked up a small Bible.

"What sort of story would you like first?" she asked, as she slowly turned the leaves.

"One 'bout Abraham, 'cause he 'most killed somebody," said Toddie, eagerly.

"Oh, no," said Budge; "one about Jesus, because *He* was always good to everybody."

"Dear child," exclaimed Mrs. Burton, "goodness always makes people nice, doesn't it?"

"Yes," said Budge, "'cept when they talk about it to little boys. Say, Aunt Alice, what makes good folks always die?"

"Because the Lord needs them, I suppose, Budge," said Mrs. Burton.

"Then don't He need *me?*" asked Budge, with a most pathetic look of inquiry.

"Certainly, dear," said Mrs. Burton; "but he wants you to make other people happy first. A great many good people are left in the world for the same reason."

"Then why couldn't Jesus be left?" said Budge. "*He* could make people happier than every one else put together."

"You'll understand why when you grow older," said Mrs. Burton.

"I wish I'd hurry up about it and grow then," said Budge. "Why can't little boys grow just like little flowers do?—just be put in the ground and watered and hoed? Our 'sparagus grows half-a-foot in a day almost."

"You's a dyty (dirty) boy to want to be put in the ground, Budge," said Toddie, "an' I isn't goin' to play wif you any more. Mamma says I mustn't play wif dyty little boys."

"Dirty boy yourself!" retorted Budge. "*You* like to play in the dirt, only you cry whenever anybody comes with water to put on you. Say, Aunt Alice, how long does people have to stay in the ground when they die before they go to heaven?"

"Three days, I suppose, Budge," said Mrs. Burton.

"'Cause that's the way it was with Jesus!"

"Yes, dear."

"And then does everybody that the Lord loves go up to heaven?"

"Yes, dear."

"Well, papa says some folks believe that dead people never go to heaven."

"Never mind what they believe, Budge—you believe what you are taught," said Mrs. Burton.

"But I'd like to know for sure."

"So you will, some day."

"I wish 'twould be pretty quick about it then," said Budge. "Now tell us a story."

Mrs. Burton drew the children nearer her as she reopened the Bible, when she discovered, to her surprise, that Toddie was crying.

"I hazhn't talked a bit for ever so long!" he exclaimed, in a high pathetic tremolo.

"What do you want to say, Toddie?" asked Mrs. Burton.

"*I* know all 'bout burying folks—that's what," said Toddie; "mamma tolded me all 'bout it one time, she did. An' yeshterday me and Budgie had a funelal all by ourselves. We found a dear little dead byde (bird). An' we w'apped it up in a piesh of paper, 'cause a baking-powder box wazn't biz enough for a coffin, an' we dugged a little grave, an' we knelted down an' said a little prayer, an' ashked the Lord to take it up to hebben, an' then we put dyte in the grave an' planted little flowers all over it —that's what."

"Yes, an' we put a little stone at the head of the grave, too, just like big dead folks," said Budge. "We couldn't find one with any writin' on it, but I went home and got a picture-book, an' cut out a little picture of a bird, an' stuck it on the stone with some tar that I picked out of the groceryman's wagon-wheel, so that when the angel that takes spirits to heaven comes along, it can see there's a dead little birdie there waiting for him."

"Yesh, an' little bydie ishn't like us—'twon't have to wunner how it'll feel to hazh wings when it gets to be a angel, 'cause 'twas all used to wings 'fore it dieded."

"Birds don't go——" began Mrs. Burton, intending to correct the children's views as to the future state of the animal kingdom, when there flashed through her mind some of the wonderings of her own girlish days, and the inability of her riper experience to answer them, so she again postponed, and with a renewed sense of its vastness, the duty of reforming the opinions of her nephews on things celestial At about the same time her cook sought an interview, and complained of the absence of two silver tablespoons. Mrs. Burton went into the mingled despondency, suspicion, and anger which is the frequent condition of all American women who are unfortunate enough to have servants.

"Where is the chambermaid?" she asked.

"An' ye's needn't to be a-suspectin' av *her*," said the cook; "it's them av yer own family that I'm thinkin' hez tuk 'em." And the cook glared suggestively upon the boys. Mrs. Burton accepted the hint.

"Boys," said she, "have either of you taken any of auntie's spoons for anything?"

"No," answered Toddie, promptly; while Budge looked very saintly and shy, as if he knew something that, through delicacy of feeling and not fear, he shrank from telling.

"What is it, Budge?" asked Mrs. Burton.

"Why, you see," said Budge, in the sweetest of tones, "we wanted something yesterday to dig the grave of the birdie with, an' we couldn't think of anything else so nice as spoons. There was plenty of ugly old iron ones lyin' around, but birdies are so sweet an' nice that I wouldn't have none of them. An' the dinner dishes was all lyin' there, with the big silver spoons on top of 'em, so I just got two of 'em—they wasn't washed yet, but we washed 'em real clean, so's to be real nice about everything, so that if the little birdie's spirit was lookin' at us it wouldn't be disgusted."

"And where are the spoons now?" demanded Mrs. Burton, oblivious to all the witchery of the child's spirit and appearance.

"I dunno," said Budge, becoming an ordinary boy in an instant.

"*I* doeszh," said Toddie; "I put 'em somewherezh, so when we wanted to play housh nexsht time we wouldn't have to make b'lieve little sticks was spoons."

"Show me immediately where they are," commanded Mrs. Burton, rising from her chair.

"Then will you lend 'em to us nexsht time we playzh housh?" asked Toddie.

"No," said Mrs. Burton, with cruel emphasis.

Toddie pouted, rubbed his knuckles into his eyes, and led the way to the rear of the garden, where, in a hollow in the base of an old apple-tree, were the missing spoons. Wondering whether other valuable property might not be there, Mrs. Burton cautiously and with a stick examined the remaining contents of the hole, and soon discovered one of her damask napkins.

"*Thatch* goin' to be our table-cloff," explained Toddie, "an' that"—this, as an unopened pot of French mustard was unearthed—"is pizzyves" (preserves).

Mrs. Burton placed her property in the pocket of her apron, led her two nephews into the house, seated them with unnecessary violence upon a sofa, shut the doors with considerable noise, drew a chair close to the prisoners, and said:

"Now, boys, you are to be punished for taking auntie's things out of the house without permission."

"Don't *want* to be shpynkted!" screamed Toddie, in a tone which seemed an attempt at a duet between a saw-filer and an ungreased wagon-wheel.

"You're not to be whipped," continued Mrs. Burton, "but you *must* learn not to touch things without permission. I think that to go without your dinners would help you to remember that what you have done is naughty."

"I'zhe 'most starved to deff," exclaimed Toddie, bursting out crying. (N.B.—Breakfast has been finished but a scant hour.)

"Then I will put you in an empty room, and keep you there until you are sure you can remember."

Toddie shrieked as if enduring the thousand tortures of the Chinese executioner, and Budge looked as unhappy as if he were a young man in love and in the throes of reluctant poesy; but Mrs. Burton led them both to the attic.

and into an empty room, placed chairs in two corners, set a boy in each chair, and said :

"Now, don't either of you move out of a chair. Just sit still and think how naughty you've been. In an hour or two I'll come back, and see if you think you can be good boys hereafter."

As Mrs. Burton left the room, she was followed by a shriek that seemed to pierce the solid walls and be heard over half the earth. But turning hastily, she saw that Toddie, from whom it had proceeded, had neither fallen out of his chair, nor been seized by an epileptic fit, nor stung by some venomous insect ; so she closed the door, locked it, softly placed a chair against it, sat down softly and listened. There was silence after the several minutes required by Toddie to weary of his crying, and then Mrs. Burton heard the following conversation :

"Tod!"

"What?"

"We ought to do *some*thing!"

"Chop Aunt Alice into little shnips of bitsh—thatsh what I fink would be nysh."

"That would be dreadful naughty," said Budge, "after we've bothered her so! We ought to do something good, just like big folks when they've been bad."

"What doezh big folks do?" asked Toddie.

"Well, they read the Bible an' go to church," said

Budge. "But you an' me can't go to church, 'cos 'tain't Sunday, and we ain't got no Bible, and we wouldn't know how to read it if we had."

"Then don't letsh do noffin' but be awful mad," said the unrepentant Toddie. "I'll tell you what we can do" (this after a short pause): "Lets do like that Maggydalen that mamma's got a picture of, and that was bad an' got sorry; letsh look awful doleful and cwosh See me."

Toddie apparently gave an illustration of what he thought to be the proper penitential countenance and attitude, for Budge exclaimed:

"I don't think *that* would look nice at all; it makes you look like a dead puppy-dog with his head turned to one side. *I'll* tell you what; we can't read Bibles like big folks, but we can tell stories out of the Bible, an' that's bein' just as good as if we read 'em."

"Oh, yes," said Toddie, repenting at once; "let's. I want to be good just *awful.*"

"Well, what shall we tell about?" asked Budge.

"'Bout when Jesus was a little boy," said Toddie, "for *he* was *awful* good."

"No," said Budge; "we've been naughty, an' we must tell about somebody that was awful naughty. I think old Pharaoh's about the thing."

"Aw wright," said Toddie, "tell us 'bout him."

"Well, once there was a bad old king down in Egypt,

that had all the Izzyrelites there an' made 'em work, an' when they didn't work he had 'em banged. But that dear little bit of a Moses, that lived in a basket in the river, grew up to be a man, an' he just killed one of Pharaoh's bad bangers, an' then he skooted and hid. An' the Lord saw that he was the kind of man that was good for something, so he told him he wanted him to make Pharaoh let the poor Izzyrelites go where they wanted to. So Moses went and told old Pharaoh. An' Pharaoh said, 'No, you don't.' Then Moses went an' told the Lord, an' the Lord got awful angry, and turned all the water in the river into blood."

"My!" said Toddie. "Then if anybody wanted to look all bluggy, all he had to do was to go in bathing, wasn't it?"

"But he wouldn't let 'em go then," continued Budge. "So the Lord made frogs hop out of all the rivers, an' mud-puddles everywhere, and they went into all the houses, an' folks couldn't keep 'em out."

"I'd just wish mamma an' me'd been in Egypt then," said Toddie; "then she couldn't make me leave my hop-toads out of doors, if the Lord wanted 'em to stay in the house. I *loves* hop-toads; I ſwallowed one the other day an' it went way down my tummuk."

"Didn't it kick in you?" asked Budge, with natural interest.

"No-o!" said Toddie. "I bited him in two fyst. But he growed togevver agin, an dzust hopped right out froe the top of my head."

"Let's see the hole he came out of," said Budge, starting across the floor.

"It all growded up again right away," said Toddie, in haste, "an' you're a bad boy to get out of your chair when Aunt Alice told you not to, and you've got to tell annuvver story about naughty folks to pay for it—gwon."

Budge returned to his chair and continued:

"An' old Pharaoh went down to Moses's house, an' said, 'Ask the Lord to make the frogs hop away, an' you can *have* your old Izzyrelites—*I* don't want 'em.' So the Lord done it, and all the glad old Pharaoh was, was only because he got rid of 'em; an' he kept the Izzyrelites some more. Then the Lord thought he'd fix 'em, sure, so he turned all the dirt into nasty bugs."

"What did the little boys do then that wanted dirt to make mud-pies of?" asked Toddie.

"Well, the bugs was only made out of *dry* dirt," exclaimed Budge; "just dust like we kick up in the street, you know."

"Oh," said Toddie, "I wonder if any of them was totato-bugs?"

"I dunno," said Budge, "but some of 'em was the kind that mammas catch with fine combs after their little boys have been playing with dirty people's children. An' Pharaoh's smart men, that thought they could do everything, found they couldn't make them bugs."

"Why," said Toddie, "did Pharaoh want some more of 'em?"

"No-o-o, I s'pose not," said Budge. "Well, he stayed bad, so he had to catch it again. The Lord sent whole swarms of flies to Egypt, and there wasn't any musquito-nets in that country either. An' then Pharaoh got good again, and the Lord took the flies away, an' Pharaoh got bad again, so the Lord made all the horses and cows awful sick and they all died."

"Then couldn't Pharaoh go out ridin' at all?" asked Toddie.

"No," said Budge, "he had to walk, even if he wanted to get to the depot in an awful hurry. An' it made him so mad that he said the Izzyrelites shouldn't go anyhow. So Moses took a handful of ashes and threw it up in the air before Pharaoh, an' everybody in all Egypt got sore with boils right away."

"Ow!" said Toddie, "I had some nashty boils oncesh, but I didn't know ashes made 'em; I'll 'member that."

"An' Pharaoh said 'No!' again, just as cross as the papa of that nice lady that Peter Gray wanted to marry, so he got some *more* bothers. The Lord made great big lumps of ice tumble down out of heaven, and he made the thunder go bang and the lightning ran around the ground like our fizzers did last Fourth of July, and it spoiled all the growing things."

"Strawberries?" queried Toddie.

"Yes."

"An' dear little panzhies?'

"Yes."

"Poo' old Pharo'!" sighed Toddie. "Gwon."

"Then Pharaoh's friends began to tell him he was bein a goose, thinkin' he could be stronger than the Lord, an' Pharaoh kind o' thought so himself. So he told Moses that the men-folks of the Izzyrelites might go away if they wanted to, but nobody else."

"Mean old fing!" said Toddie. "Who did he fink was goin' to cook fings an' go to school?"

"I dunno," said Budge; "but I guess he had a chance to think about it, for the Lord made whole crowds of locusts come. Them's grasshoppers, you know, an' they ate up everything in all the gardens, an' the folks got half crazy about it."

"*Then* I guesh they didn't tell their little boysh that they mushn't kill grasshoppers, like mamma doesh. Wish *I'd* have been there! What did he do then?"

"Oh, he was a selfish old pig, just like he was before," said Budge; "so the Lord said, 'Moses, just hold your hand up to the sky a minute.' An' Moses did it, and then it got darker in Egypt than it is in our coal-bin. Folks couldn't see anything anywhere, and wherever they was when it growed dark, they had to stay for three whole days and nights."

"Gwacious!" said Toddie. "Wouldn't it be drefful if Moses was to go an' hold his hand up in the sky while we're a-sittin' in thezhe chairzh! Mebbe he will; let's holler for Aunt Alice!"

"Oh, he *can't* do it *now*," said Budge, "'cause he's dead. Besides that *we* ain't keepin' any Izzyrelites from doin' what they want to. Old Pharaoh got awful frightened then, an' told Moses he might take all the people away, but they mustn't take their things with 'em—the selfish old fellow! But Moses knew how hard the poor Izzyrelites had to work for the few things they had, so he said they wouldn't go unless they could carry everything they owned. An' that made Pharaoh mad, an' he said, 'Get out If I catch you here again I'll kill you!' An' Moses said, 'Don't trouble yourself; you won't see *me* again unless you want me.'"

"Shouldn't think he would," said Toddie, "Nobody goin' to vizhit kings dzust to have their heads cutted off. Even our shickens knows enough not to come to Mike when he wants to cut their heads off. Gwon!"

"Well, then the Lord told Moses somethin' that must just have made him feel *awful*. He told him that next night every biggest boy in every family was goin' to be killed by an angel. *My!* ain't I glad I didn't live there then! I'd like to see an angel, but not if *that's* what he wants to do with me. What would you do if an angel wazh to kill me, Tod?"

"I'd have your marbles," said Toddie, promptly, "and the goat-carriage would be all mine. Gwon!"

"Well, the Lord told Moses about it, an' Moses told the folks; an' he told 'em all to kill a little lamb, an' dip their fingers in the blood, an' make a cross on their door-posts, so when the angel came along an' saw it he wouldn't kill the biggest boy in *their* houses. An' that night down came the angel, an' everybody woke up an' cried *awful*—worse than you did when you fell down-stairs the other day—because all the biggest boys an' girls died. You couldn't go anywhere without hearin' papas an' mammas cryin'."

"Did they all have funerals then?" asked Toddie.

"Of course," said Budge.

"Gwacious!" said Toddie. "Then the little 'Gyptian boys that didn't get killed could look at deaders all day long! What did Pharo' do 'bout it then?"

"He sent right after Moses an' his brother, in a hurry, an' he told 'em that he'd been a bad king—just as if they didn't know that already. An' he told 'em to take all the Izzyrelites, an' all their things, an' go right straight away

—he was in such a hurry that he didn't even invite Moses to the funeral, though he had a dead biggest boy himself. An all the Egyptian people came too, and begged the Izzyrelites to hurry an' go—they didn't see what they was waitin' for. They was so glad to get rid of 'em that they lent 'em anything they wanted."

"Pies an' cakes?" asked Toddie.

"No!" said Budge, contemptuously. "You don't s'pose folks that's goin' off travelin' for forty years is goin' to think about eatin' first thing, do you? They borrowed clothes, an' money, an' everything else they could get, an' left the Egyptians *awful* poor. An' off they started."

"Did they have a 'scursion train?" asked Toddie.

"No," said Budge, "All the excursion trains in the world couldn't have held such lots of people. They rode on camels and donkeys, but lots of 'em walked."

"I don't think *that* was a *bit* of fun," said Toddie.

"You *would* have," said Budge, "if you'd always had to work like everything. Don't you 'member how once when mamma made *you* work, an' carry away all the blocks you brought up on the piazza from the new buildin'? You walked way off to the village to get rid of it."

"Ye—es," drawled Toddie, "but I knew I'd be rided back when they came to look for me. *Then* what did they do?"

"They started to travel to a nice country that the Lord

had told Moses about, an' they got along till they came to a pretty big ocean where there wasn't any ferry-boats—I don't see what Moses took 'em to such a place as *that* for, unless the Lord wanted to show 'em that no ferry-boats couldn't get the best of *Him*—when all of a sudden they saw an awful lot of dust bein' kicked up behind 'em, an' somebody said that Pharaoh was a-comin'."

"Sould fink he'd seen 'nough of 'em," said Toddie. "Did he come down to the boat to wave his hanafitch (handkerchief) good-by at 'em?"

"No," said Budge. "He knew there wasn't any boats there, and so he came to take 'em back again an' make 'em work some more."

"Sould fink he'd be afraid the Lord would kill him next," said Toddie.

"P'r'aps he did," said Budge. "But then you see he was awful lazy, an' didn't like to work for himself—papa says there's lots of folks that would rather be killed than to work."

"Then what do they do?" asked Toddie. "*They* can't catch any Izzyrelites to work for 'em can they?"

"No," said Budge, "but they do what the Izzyrelites did themselves—they borrow other people's money. Well, when the folks saw that *'twas* Pharaoh a-comin', they began to grunt, an' pitch into poor Moses, an' told him he ought to be ashamed of hisself to bring 'em away off there to be killed, when they might have died in Egypt without havin' to walk so far. But Moses said: 'Do be quiet: the Lord is managing this thing.' Then the Lord said: 'Moses, just lift up your cane an' point across the water with it!' An' the minute Moses did that the water of that ocean went way up on one side, and way up on the other side—just like it does in the bath-tub sometimes when we're splashin', you know—and there was a path right through the bottom of that ocean. An' the people just skooted right along it."

"Did they put on their rubbers fust?" asked Toddie. "'Cause if they didn't there must have been lots of little boys spanked when they got across for gettin' their shoes muddy."

"I don't know about that," said Budge, after a slight pause for reflection. "I must 'member to ask papa about that. But when they all got over they began to grumble some more, for along came Pharaoh's army right after 'em."

"*I* fink they was a lot of good-for-nothing cry-babies," said Toddie.

"Huh!" grunted Budge. "I guess *you'd* have yowled if you'd have been trudgin' along through the mud ever so long an' then seen some soldiers an' chariots an' spears an' bows an' arrows comin' to kill you. But the Lord knew just how to manage—He always did. Papa says He *always* comes in when you think He can't. He said to Moses, 'Just lift up your cane an' point it across the ocean again, will you?' An' Moses did it, an' *down* came that big fence of water on both sides *ker-swosh!* An' it drownded old Pharaoh an' the whole good-for-nothin' lot."

"Then did the Izzyrelites go to cryin' some more," asked Toddie.

"Not much!" said Budge, "They all got together an' had a big sing."

"*I* know what they sung," said Toddie. "They all sung 'TurnbackPharo'sarmyhallelujah.'"

"No, they didn't," said Budge. "They sung that spendid thing mamma sings sometimes, 'Sound the—loud tim—brel o'er—Egypt's—Egypt's dark——'"

Budge had with great difficulty repeated the line of the glorious old anthem, and he finally broke down and burst out crying.

"What's you cryin' about?" asked Toddie. "Is you playin' you's an Izzyrelite?"

"No," said Budge; "but whenever I think about that song, something comes up in my throat and *makes* me cry."

"The door of the room flew open, there was a rustle and a hurried tread, and Mrs. Burton, her own face full of tears, snatched Budge to her breast, and kissed him repeatedly, while Toddie remarked:

"When fings come up in *my* throat I just *fwallows* em.'

Mrs. Burton conducted her nephews to the parlor floor, and said:

"Now, little boys, it's nearly lunch time, and I am going to have you nicely washed and dressed, so that if any one comes in you will look like little gentlemen."

"Ain't we to be punished any more for bein' bad?" asked Budge.

"No," said Mrs. Burton, kindly, "I'm going to trust you to remember and be good."

"*That* isn't what bothers me," said Budge; "I told a great, long Bible story to Tod up-stairs, so's to be like big folks when they get bad, as much as I could, and *he* didn't tell *any'*; I don't think he's got his punish"

"He may tell his to-night, after Uncle Harry gets home," said Mrs. Burton.

"An' sit in a chair in the corner of the up-stairs room?" asked Budge.

"I hardly think that will be necessary this time," answered the lady.

"Then I don't think you punish fair a 'bit,'" said Budge, with an aggrieved pout.

"I'll be dzust as sad as I *can* 'bout it Budge," said Toddie, with a brotherly kiss.

The boys were led off by the chambermaid to be dress

ed, and Mrs. Burton seated herself and devoted herself to earnest thought. Time was flying, her husband had been between dark and breakfast-time most exasperatingly solicitous as to the success of his wife's theories of government, and not even her wondrous genius of self-defense had prevailed against him. She felt that so far she had been steadily vanquished. Her husband had told her in other days that it was always so with the best of generals in their first engagements, and she determined that if men had snatched victory from the jaws of defeat, she should be able to do so as well. She determined that she would; her desperation at the thought of a long lifetime of "I told you so's" from her husband made her determine that no discomfort should prevent the most earnest endeavour for success. Like many another general, however, she realized by the memory of her defeats that will is not ability, and that the most accurate perception of what results should be is attained by faculties very different from those which can devise the means by which results are to be assured.

The lunch-bell aroused her from what finally became a reverie in the valley of humiliation, and she found awaiting her at the table her nephews—Budge in a jaunty sailor-suit, and Toddie in a clean dress and an immaculate white apron. An old experience caused her to promptly end some researches of Toddie's, instituted to discover whether his aunt's dishes were really "turtle-pyates," and an attempt by Budge to drop oysters in the mouth of the dog Jerry, as he had seen his uncle do with bread-crusts in the morning, was forcibly brought to a close Beyond the efforts alluded to, the children did nothing worse at the table than, or even so bad as people in good society often do.

CHAPTER III.

After lunch was concluded, Mrs. Burton said:

"Now, boys, this is Aunt Alice's reception-day. I will probably have several calls, and every one will want to know about that dear little baby, and you must be here to tell them. So you must keep yourselves very neat and clean. I know you wouldn't like to see any dirty people in my parlor!"

"Hatesh to shtay in parlors," said Toddie. "Wantsh to go an' get some jacks," ("Jack-in-the-pulpit"—a swamp plant).

"Not to-day," said Mrs. Burton, kindly, but firmly. "No one with nice white aprons on ever goes for jacks. What would you think if you saw *me* in a swampy, muddy place, with a nice white apron on, hunting for jacks?"

"Why, I'd fink you could bring home more'n me, 'cause *your* apron would hold the mosht" said Toddie.

"*I'll* tell you what," said Budge, calling Toddie into a corner and whispering earnestly to him. The exquisite purity of Budge's expression of countenance and the tender shyness with which he avoided her gaze when he noticed that it was upon him, caused Mrs. Burton to instinctively turn her head away, out of respect for what she believed to be a childish secret of some very tender order. Glancing at the couple again for only a second, she saw that Toddie, too, seemed rather less matter-of-fact than usual. Finally both boys started out of the door-way, Budge turning and remarking with inflections simply angelic:

"We'll be back pretty soon, Aunt Alice."

Mrs. Burton proceeded to dress; she idly touched her piano, and finally one lady after another called, and occupied her time. Suddenly, while trying to form a proper impression upon a very dignified lady of the old school, both boys marched into the parlor from the dining-room. Mrs. Burton motioned them violently away, for Budge's trowsers and Toddie's apron were as dirty as they well could be. Neither boy saw the visitor, however, for she was hidden by one of the wings which held the folding-doors, so both tramped up to their aunt, while Budge exclaimed:

"Folks don't go to heaven the *second* day, anyhow, for we just dug up the bird to see, an' he was there yet just the same."

"And there wazh lots of little ants there wiv him," said Toddie. "Is that 'cause they want to go to hebben, too, and wantsh somebody wiv wingsh to help 'em up?"

"Budge!" exclaimed Mrs. Burton, in chilling tones, "how did all this dirt come on your clothes?"

"Why, you see," said the boy, edging up confidentially to his aunt, and resting his elbows on her knee as he looked up into her face, "I couldn't bear to put the dear little birdie in the ground again without saying another little prayer. And I forgot to brush my knees off."

"Toddie," said Mrs. Burton, "*you* couldn't have knelt down with your stomach and breast. How did you get your nice white apron so dirty?"

Toddie looked at the apron and then at his aunt—looked at a picture or two, and then at the piano—followed the cornice-line with his eye, seemed suddenly to find what he was looking for, and replied:

"Do *you* fink that apron's dyty? Well, *I* don't. Tell you whatsh the matter wif it—I fink the white's dropped off."

"Go into the kitchen," commanded Mrs. Burton, and both boys departed with heavy pouts where pretty lips should have been. Half an hour later their uncle, who had come home early with the laudable desire of meeting some of his wife's lady acquaintances, found his nephew Toddie upon the scaffolding of an unfinished residence, half way between his own residence and the railway station. Remembering the story, dear to all makers of school reading-books, of the boy whose sailor father saw him perched upon the main yard, Mr. Burton stood beneath the scaffolding and shouted to Toddie:

"Jump!"

"I can't!" screamed Toddie.

"Jump!" shouted Mr. Burton, with increased energy.

"Tell you I can't," repeated Toddie. "Wezh playin' Tower of Babel, an' hazh had our talks made different like the folks did then, an' when I tell's Budge to bring bricksh, he only bringzh mortar, an' when I wantsh mortar he bringzh bricksh. An' then we talksh like you an' Aunt Alice did yestuday at the table."

"Yes," said Budge, appearing from the inside of the building with an armful of blocks. "Just listen." And the young man chattered for a moment or two in a dialect never even dimly hinted at except by a convention of monkeys.

Mr. Burton cautiously climbed the ladder, brought down one boy at a time, then kissed them both and shook them soundly, after which the three wended homeward, the boys having sawdust on every portion of their clothes not already soiled by dirt, and most of Mrs Burton's callers meeting the party *en route.*

Mr. Burton found his wife most brilliantly conversational, but as averse to talking about her nephews as if they were pre-adamite remains and she were a stickler for the literal integrity of the book of Genesis. The exercise which these young men had been compelled to take in their emulation of the architects of the incomplete building on the plain of Shinar gave them excellent appetites and silenced tongues; but after his capacity had been tested to the uttermost, Budge remarked:

"It's time for Tod to do *his* punishment now, Aunt Alice; don't you know?"

Mrs. Burton winked at her husband and nodded, approvingly to Budge.

"Come, Tod," said Budge, "you must tell *your* awful sad story now, an' feel bad."

"Guesh I'll tell 'bout Peter Gray," said Toddie; "thatsh awful sad."

"Who was Peter Gray?" asked Mrs. Burton.

"He's a dzentleman that a dyty little boy in the nekshst street to us sings 'bout," said Toddie, "only I don't sing 'bout him—I only tellsh it—it's dzust as sad that-a-way."

"Go on," said Budge.

"Once was a man," said Toddie, with great solemnity and bated breath, "an' his name was *Peter* Gray. An' he loved a lady. An' he saysh to her papa, 'I wantsh to marry your little gyle (girl).' An' what you fink that papa said? He said, 'No!'" (this with tremendous emphasis). "That izhn't as hard as he said it, eiver, but it's azh hard as I can say it. It's puffikly dzedful when Jimmy sings it. An' Peter Gray felt awful bad then, an' he went Wesht, to buy the shkinzh that comes off of animals an' fings, though how that made him feel nicer Jimmy don't sing 'bout. An' bad Injuns caught him an' pulled his hair off, djust like ladies pull theirsh off sometimezh. An' when that lady heard 'bout it, it made her feel so bad that she went to bed an' died. Thatsh all. Uncle Harry, ain't *you* got to be punished for somefin', so you can tell ush a story?

"It's time little boys were in bed, now," said Mrs. Burton, arising, and taking Toddie in her arms

"Oh, dear!" said Budge. "I wishes I was a little boy in China, an' just gettin' up."

"So does I," said Toddie; "'cause then you would have a tay-al on your head, an' I could pull it!"

The boys retired, and Mrs. Burton broke her reticence so far as to tell her husband the story she had heard in the morning, and to insist that he was to arise early enough in the morning to unearth the buried bird and throw it away.

"It's perfectly dreadful," said she, "that those children should be encouraged in making trifling applications of holy truths, and I am determined, as far as possible, to prevent the effects by removing the causes."

And her husband put on a most discouraging smile, and shook his head profoundly.

The sun of the next morning arose at the outrageously unfashionable hour that he affects in June; but Mrs. Burton was up before him. Her husband had attended a town-meeting the night before, and the forefathers of the hamlet had been so voluble that Mr. Burton had not returned home until nearly midnight. He needed rest, and his wife determined that he should sleep as long as possible; but there were things dearer to her than even the comfort of her husband, and among these were the traditions she had received concerning things mystical and holy. She had an intuition that her nephews would promptly test the central hope of the Christian world by examining the grave of the bird they had interred two days before, and she dreaded to listen to the literal conversation and comments that would surely follow. Had the bird been a human being, the remarks of its tender-hearted little friends would have seemed anything but materialistic to Mrs. Burton; but it was only a bird, and the lady realized that to answer questions as to the soullessness of an innocent being and the comparative value of characterlessness men and women was going to be no easy task. She therefore perfected a plan which should be just and righteous to all concerned; she would arouse her husband only when she heard her nephews moving; then she would engage the young men in conversation while her husband rifled the grave. She would have saved considerable trouble by locking the young men in their chamber and allowing her husband to slumber to his body's content; but having failed to remove the key on the advent of the boys, they had found use for it themselves, and no questioning had been able to discover its whereabouts. Meanwhile the boys were quiet, and Mrs. Burton devoted the peaceful moments to laying out the day in such a manner as to have the least possible trouble from her nephews, and to impress most fully upon them that individuality which she reluctantly admitted had so far been conquered rather than conquering.

A violent kicking at the front door and some vigorous rings of the bell aroused the lady from her meditation and her husband from his dreams, while the dog Terry, who usually slept on the inner mat at the front door, began to howl piteously.

"Goodness!" growled Mr. Burton, rubbing his eyes, as his wife pulled the bell-cord leading to the servant's room. "To whom do we owe money in Hillcrest?"

"Oh, I'm afraid Helen is worse, or the baby is poorly!" exclaimed Mrs. Burton, opening the chamber-window, and shouting, "Who is there?"

"Me," answered a voice easily recognizable as that of Budge.

"Me, too!" screamed a thinner but equally familiar voice.

"We've got something *awful* lovely to tell you, Aunt Alice," shouted Budge. "Let us in, quick!"

"Lovelier than cake or pie or candy!" screamed Toddie.

One of the servants hurried down the stairs, the door opened, light footsteps hurried up the steps, and the dog Terry, pausing for no morning caress from his master, hurried under the bed for refuge, from which locality he expressed his apprehension in a dismal falsetto. Then, with a tramp which only children can execute, and which horses cannot approach in noisiness, came Budge and Toddie. Arrived at their aunt's chamber-door, each boy tried to push the other away, that he might himself tell the story of which both were full. At last, from the outer edge of the door-jamb, against which his face was being tightly pressed by his brother's, Toddie shouted:

"Dear little bydie's gone to hebben."

"Yes," said Budge, relaxing his brotherly effort, "the angels took him away."

"An' the little ants all went to hebben wif him," said Toddie.

"Only the angels didn't take the gravestone, too," said Budge. "Say, Aunt Alice, what's the use of gravestones after folks is gone to heaven?"

"*I* know," said Toddie, with ineffable scorn; "I fought *every* body knowed *that;* it's so's folks know where to plant lovaly flowers for their angel what was in the grave too look down at."

"Now," said Budge, with the air of a champion of a newly discovered doctrine, "I'm jist goin' to ask papa who the folks are that don't believe deaders go to heaven. *I'll* jist tell 'em what geese they are."

"Angels *is* dzust like birdies, isn't they, Aunt Alice?" said Toddie, "'cause they've got wingsh an' clawsh, too."

"How do you know they have claws?" asked Mr. Burton.

"'Cause I saw their scratch-holes in the dyte at the grave," said Toddie. "They was dzust little *bits* of scratchy cracks like little bydies make; I guesh they was little baby-angels."

Mr. Burton winked at his wife, who was looking greatly mystified, and he uttered the single monosyllable:

"Cats."

"How did you get out of the house, children?" asked Mr. Burton.

"Jumped out of one of the kitchen windows," said Budge, "but it was so high from the ground that we couldn't get in again that way. And *I* think it's breakfast-time—we've been up 'bout two hours."

"Now's the time for orthodox teaching, my dear," suggested Mr. Burton; "physiologists say that the mind is more active when the stomach's empty."

"Thank you," said Mrs. Burton, starting for the kitchen, "but the minds of those boys are too active even on full stomachs."

Breakfast was on the table in due time, and the boys showed a toothsome appreciation of it. After they were reasonably satisfied, however, Budge remarked:

"Aunt Alice, how much longer do you suppose we can live without seeing that dear little sister-baby?"

"Dear little *girl* sister-baby," said Toddie, by way of correction.

"Oh, quite a good while, I guess," said Mrs. Burton. "I know you love it and your mamma too much to make either of them any trouble, and both of them are quite feeble yet. You love them better than you do yourself, don't you?"

"Certainly," said Budge. "That's why I want to see 'em so awful much."

"I fink it's awful mean for little sishterzh not to have their budders to play wif," said Toddie.

"Well," said Mrs. Burton, "I will think about it, and if I feel sure that you will both be *very* good, we will go there to-day."

"Oh, my!" said Budge, "we'll be our very goodest. I'll tell you what, Tod; we'll have a Sunday-school right after breakbux—*that'll* be good."

"I know something gooder than that," said Toddie.

"We'll play Daniel in the lion's den, and you be the king an' take me out. That's a good deal gooder than dzust playin' Sunday-school; 'caush takin' folks away from awful bitey lions is a gooder fing than dzust singin' an' prayin', like they do in Sunday-school."

"Another frightful fit of heterodoxy to be overcome, my dear," observed Mr. Burton. "That dreadful child is committed to the doctrine of the superior efficacy of works over faith."

"I shall tell him the story of Daniel correctly, then," said Mrs. Burton, "and error will be sure to fly from the appearance of truth"

Mr. Burton took his departure for the day, and while his wife busied herself in household management, the children discussed the etiquette of the promised visit.

"Tell you what, Tod," said Budge, "we ought to take her presents, anyhow. That was one of the lovaly things about Jesus being a little baby once. You know those shepherds came an' brought him lots of presents."

"What letsh take her?" asked Toddie.

"Well," said Budge, "the shepherds carried money and things that smelled sweet, so I guess that's what we ought to do."

"Aw wight," said Toddie, "'cept houzh we goin' to get 'em?"

"We can go into the house *very* softly when we get

home, you know," said Budge, "an' shake some pennies out of our savings-bank; them'll do for the money. Then for things that smell sweet we can get flowers out of the garden."

"That'll be dzust a-givin' her fings that's at home already. I fink 'twould be nicer to carry her somefing from here, just as if *we* were comin' from where we took care of the sheep."

"Tell you what," said Budge, "let's tease Aunt Alice for pennies. We ought to have thought about it before Uncle Harry went away."

"Oh, yes!" said Toddie, "an' there's a bottle of smelly stuff in Aunt Alice's room; we'll get some of *that*. Shall we ask for it, or dzust make b'lieve it's ours?"

"Let's be honest 'bout it," said Budge. "It's wicked to hook things."

"Twouldn't be hookin' if we took it for that lovaly little sister-baby, would it?" asked Toddie. "'Sides, I want to s'prise Aunt Alice and everybody wif the lots of presentsh I makesh to the dear ittle fing"

"Oh! *I'll* tell you what," said Budge, forgetting the presents entirely in his rapture over a new idea. "You know how bright the point of the new lightning-rod on our house is? Well, we'll make b'lieve that's the Star in the East, an' it's showin' us where to come to find the baby."

"Oh, yes!" exclaimed Toddie. "An' maybe Aunt

Alice 'll carry us on her back, and then we'll make believe we're ridin' camels, like the shepherds in the picture we had Christmas, an' tore up to make menageries of."

The appearance of a large grasshopper directly in front of the boys ended the conversation temporarily, for both started in chase of it, with the usual unsuccessful result.

Half an hour later both boys straggled into the house, panting and dusty, and flung themselves upon the floor, when their aunt, with that weakness peculiar to the woman who is not also a mother, asked them where they had been, why they were out of breath, how they came by so much dust on their clothes, and why they were so cross. Budge replied, with a heavy sigh:

"Big folks don't know much about little folkses, troubles."

"Bad old hoppergrass, djust kept a goin' wherever he wanted to, an' never comed under my hat," complained Toddie,

"Perhaps he knew it would not be best for you to have him, Toddie," said Mrs. Burton. "What would you have done with him if you had succeeded in catching him?"

"Tookted his hind hoppers off," said Toddie, promptly.

"Why, how dreadful!" exclaimed Mrs. Burton. "What would you have done that for?"

"So's he'd fly," said Toddie. "The idea of anybody wif wings goin' awound on their hoppers—how'd *you* like it if *I* had wings, an' only trotted and jumped instead of flied?"

"My dear little boy," said Mrs. Burton, taking her nephew in her lap, "you must know that it's very wrong to hurt animals in that way. They are just as the Lord made them, and just as he wants them to be."

"*All* animals?" asked Toddie.

"Certainly," answered Mrs. Burton.

"Then what for doesh you catch pitty little mices in traps an' kill 'em?" asked Toddie, with widely opening eyes.

"Because they're very troublesome," said Mrs. Burton. "And even troublesome people have to be punished when they meddle with other people's things."

"*We* know that, I guess," interposed Budge, with a sigh.

"But," said Mrs. Burton, hurrying forward to her point, "the animals have nerves and flesh and blood and bones, just like little boys do, and are just the way the Lord made them."

"I'll *look* for a hoppergrass's blood next time I pull one's legsh off," said Toddie.

"Don't" said Mrs. Burton; "you must believe what aunty tells you, and you musn't trouble the poor things at all. Why, Toddie, there are real smart men, real good men that everybody respects, that have spent their whole lives in study with bits of insects, like grasshoppers and flies and bees——"

"An' never get stung?" asked Toddie. "How did they do it?"

"They don't care if they are stung," said Mrs. Burton — "they are so deeply interested in learning how animals are made. They study all kinds of animals, and try to find out why they are different from people; and they find out that some wee things, like grasshoppers, are more wonderful than any person that ever lived!"

"I should think so," said Budge. "If *I* could hop like a grasshopper, I could jump faster than any boy in the Kindergarten, an' if I could sting like a hornet, I could wallop any boy in town."

"Does they adzamine *bid* animals, too?" asked Toddie.

"Yes," said Mrs. Burton. "One of them, a Mr. Marsh, has been away out West among the dreadful Indians, just to find out what horses were like a good many years ago."

"If *I* find out all 'bout horsesh," said Toddie, "will everybody like *me?*"

"Very likely," said Mrs. Burton.

"Then I'm goin' to," said Toddie, sliding out of his aunt's lap.

"Never mind about it now, dear," said Mrs. Burton. "We are going to see mamma and the baby now. Go dress yourselves neatly, boys."

Both children started, and Mrs. Burton, who was already prepared for her trip, opened a novel, first giving herself credit for having turned at least one perverted faculty of Toddie's into its heaven-ordained channel.

"Another triumph to report to my husband," said she, with a fine air of exultation, as she opened her novel. "And yet," she continued, absent-mindedly, laying the book down again, "I believe I've found no occasion on which to report yesterday's victories!"

The boys were slow to appear; but when, finally, they came down-stairs, they presented so creditable an appearance as to call for a special compliment from their aunt. On the way to their mamma's house they were very bright, but seemed preoccupied, and they sought frequent occasions to whisper to each other.

Arrived at home, their impatience knew no restraint; and when the nurse appeared with a wee bundle, topped with a little face, and lying on a big pillow, both boys pounced upon it at once, Budge trying to crowd several pennies into the baby's rose-leaves of hands, while Toddie held to its nose a bottle labeled "Liquid Bluing;" at the same time the baby sneezed alarmingly, and a strong odor of camphor pervaded the room.

"Where *can* that camphor be?" asked the nurse. "There is nothing that Mrs. Lawrence hates so intensely!"

The New Baby. (*Page* 70.)

The baby stopped sneezing and began a pitiful wail, while Toddie hastened to pick up the bluing-bottle; then the nurse saw that upon the baby's hitherto immaculate wraps there was a large stain of a light-blue tint, and emitting a strong odor of camphor; meanwhile, Toddie had dragged upon his aunt's sacque, held his precious bottle up to his aunt's nose, and exclaimed:

"Izhn't that too baddy! Baby gropped it, and spilled mosht every bit of it on her c'ozhes an' on the floor!"

"Where did you get that camphor, Toddie?" asked Mrs. Burton, "and what *did* you bring it here for?"

"*Tizhn't* campiffer," said Toddie; "its pyfume; I got it out of a big bottle on your bureau, where you makes your hankafusses (handkerchiefs) smell sweet at. Budgie an' me done dzust what them sheep-men did when they came to Beflehem to see the dear little Jesus-baby—we brought *our* baby money an' fings that smelled sweet."

Mrs. Burton kissed Toddie, and so did the nurse; then the nurse sat on the floor, and displayed the baby's face, and then the face was shadowed from the light, and baby opened two little eyes and regarded her brothers with a stare of queenly gravity and gentleness, and the adoration expressed by the faces of the two boys was such as no old master ever put into the faces in an "Adoration of the Magi," and above them bent a face more mature but none the less suffused with tender awe. The silence seemed too holy and delightful to be broken, but Toddie finally looked up inquiringly into his aunt's face and asked:

"Aunt Alice, why don't there be a lovaly sun around her head like there is in pictures of dear little Jesus-babies?"

The quartet became human again, and the nurse offered each one of the party a five-minute interview with the mother. Mrs. Burton emerged from the sick-chamber with a face which her nephews could not help scrutinizing curiously. Budge came out with the remark that he would never worry his sweet mamma again while he lived, but Toddie exclaimed:

"If I had a little new baby I wouldn't stay in bed in dark roomsh all day long. I dzust get up an' dansh awound."

"Aunt Alice," asked Budge, on the way back to his uncle's residence, "now there's somebody else at our house to have a birthday, isn't there? When will baby sister's birthday come—how many days?"

"Three hundred and sixty-two," said Mrs. Burton.

"Goodness!" exclaimed Budge. "And how long 'fore Christmas 'll come again!"

"Nearly two hundred days," said the lady.

"Well, I think I will *die* if somebody don't have a birthday pretty soon, so I can give 'em presents," said Budge.

"Why, you dear, generous little fellow," said Mrs Burton, stooping to kiss him, "my *birthday* will come to morrow."

"Oh—h—h—h!" exclaimed Budge. "Say, Toddie——" and the remainder of the conversation was conducted in whispers, and with countenances of extreme importance. The boys even took a different road for home, Budge explaining to his aunt that they had a big secret to talk about.

Mrs. Burton stopped *en route* to ask a neighborly question or two, and arrived at home somewhat later than her nephews, and saw a horse and wagon at the door. She soon and rightly imagined that these belonged to her grocer, and she divined that the driver thereof was interviewing the Burton servants. But what a certain white mass on the ground under the horse could consist of Mrs. Burton was at a loss to conjecture, and she quickened her pace only to find the white substance aforesaid resolve itself into the neatly clothed body of her nephew, Toddie, who was lying on his back in the dirt, and contemplating the noble animal's chest with serene curiosity.

There are moments in life when dignity unbends in spite of itself, and grace of deportment becomes a thing to be loathed. Such a moment Mrs. Burton endured, as, dropping her parasol, she cautiously but firmly seized Toddie and snatched him from his dangerous position.

"Go into the house, this instant, you dirty boy!" exclaimed Mrs. Burton, with an imperious stamp of her foot.

The fear in Toddie's countenance gave place to expostulation, as he exclaimed:

"I was only dzust—"

"Go into the house this instant!" repeated Mrs. Burton.

"Ah—h—h—h!" said Toddie, beginning to cry, and rolling out his under lip as freely as if there were yards of it yet to come. "I was only studyin' how the horsie was made togevver, so 's everybody 'd 'espec' an' love *me*. Can't go to where them Injuns is, an' I fought a gushaway (grocery) man's horsie would be dzust as good. Ah—h—h!"

"There was no necessity for your lying on the ground, in your clean pique dress to do it," said Mrs. Burton.

"Ah—h—h!" said Toddie again. "I studied all the yest of him fyst, an' I couldn't hold him up so as to look under him. I tried to, an' he looked at me dzeadful crosh, an' so I didn't."

"Go right into the house and have another dress put on," said Mrs. Burton. "You know very well that nothing excuses little boys for dirtying their clothes when they can help it. When your Uncle Harry comes home, we shall have to devise some way of punishing you so that you will remember to take better care of your clothing in the future."

"Ah—h—h—h—! I hope God won't make any more horsesh, then, nor any little boys to be told to find out about 'em, then be punnissed dzust for gettin' their c'oshes a little dyty!" screamed Toddie, disappearing through the doorway, and filling the house with angry screams.

Mrs. Burton lingered for a moment upon the piazza steps, and experienced but bravely endured a spasm of sense. There forced itself upon her mind the idea that it might be possible, according to a code less erratic than that of the well-ordered household, that the soiling of garments was not the sin of all sins, and that Toddie had really been affected by her information about the noble origin and nature of the animal physique. Certainly nothing but a sincere passion for investigation could have led Toddie between the feet of a horse, and a person so absorbed in scientific pursuits might possibly be excused for being regardless of personal appearance. But, no; clean clothing ranked next to clean hearts in the Mayton family, and such acquirements as Mrs. Burton possessed she determined to lovingly transmit to her nephews so far as was in her power. But Toddie seemed really in earnest in his indignation, and she respected mistaken impressions which were honestly made, so she determined to try to console the weeping child. Going into his room, she found her nephew lying on his back, kicking, screaming, and otherwise giving vent to his rage.

"Toddie," said Mrs. Burton, "it is too bad that you should have so much trouble just after you have been to see your mamma and little sister."

"I know it!" screamed Toddie, "an' you can dzust go down-stairsh again if that's all you came to tell me."

"But, Toddie, dear," said Mrs. Burton, kneeling and smoothing the hot forehead of her nephew, "aunty wants to see you feeling comfortable again."

"Then put me back under the horsie again, so folksh 'll 'espec' me," sobbed Toddie.

"You've learned enough about the horse for to-day," said Mrs. Burton. "I'll ask your papa to teach you more when you go back home. Poor little boy, how hot your cheeks are! Aunt Alice wishes she could see you looking happy again."

Toddie stopped crying for a moment, looked at his aunt intently, sat up, put on an air of considerable importance, and finally said:

"Did Lord send you up-stairsh to tell me you was sorry for what you done to me?" asked Toddie. "Then I forgives you, only don't do that baddy way any more. If you want to put a clean dress on me, you can."

"Aunt Alice," said Budge, who had rambled into the room, "you told Uncle Harry at the breakbux table that you was goin' to tell us about Daniel to-day; don't you think it's about time to do it?"

"Oh, yes," said Toddie, hurrying his head through his clean dress, "an' how the lions yet up the bad men that made the king frow Daniel in the deep dark hole. G'won."

"There was a very good young man once whose name was Daniel," said Mrs. Burton, "and although the king made a law that nobody should pray except to the gods that his people worshiped, Daniel prayed every day to the same God that we love."

"He was up in Heaven then, like he is now, wasn t he?" said Budge.

"Oh, yes," answered Mrs. Burton.

"Then where was the other people's god?"

"Oh, on shelves and in closets, and all sorts of places," said Mrs. Burton. "They were only bits of wood and stone—idols, in fact."

"And wasn't they good?" asked Budge.

"Not at all," said Mrs. Burton.

"Well, I don't think that's very nice," said Budge, "for papa sometimes says that *I* am mamma's idol. Am I sticky or stony?"

"Certainly not, dear; he means that your mother cares a great deal for you—that is all. And Daniel prayed just as he chose and when he chose, and the people that didn't like him hurried up to the king and said, 'Just see, that young man of whom you care so much is praying to the Lord that the Jews believe in.' The king was sorry to hear this, but Daniel wouldn't tell a lie; he admitted that he prayed just as he wanted to, so the king had to order some men to throw Daniel into the den of lions. He felt very badly about it, though, for Daniel had been always very good and honest, and very good people are hard to find anywhere."

"Musht tell mamma that nexsht time she saysh *I* must be very good," said Toddie. "Gwon."

"They threw poor Daniel in among the lions," said Mrs. Burton, "and he must have felt dreadfully on the way to the den, for he knew that lions are very savage and hungry. Why, one single lion will often eat up a whole man, yet there were a great many lions in the den Daniel was taken to."

"He wouldn't make much of a supper for all of *them*, poor fellow, would he?" said Budge.

"No," said Mrs. Burton, "so he did what sensible people always do when they find themselves in trouble. He prayed. As for the king, I imagine he didn't sleep much that night. People who take the advice of others, and against their own better judgment, generally have to feel uncomfortable. At any rate, the king was awake very early in the morning, and hurried off to the den alone, and looked in, and shouted "Daniel? the Lord in whom you believe, was he strong enough to keep the lions from eating you?" And then Daniel answered the king. Think of how happy it must have made the king to hear his voice, and know he was not dead! The unkindness of the king had not made Daniel forget to be respectful, so he said: 'Oh, king, I hope you may live forever.' Then he told the king that he had not been hurt at all, and the king was very glad, and he had Daniel taken out, and then the bad men who had been the cause of Daniel being given to the lions were all thrown into the den, and the lions ate every one of them."

"*I* know why they let Daniel alone an' ate up all the other fellows," said Budge, with a noble air of comprehension.

"I felt sure you would, dear little boy," said Mrs. Burton; "but you may tell me what you think about it."

"Why, you see," said Budge, "Daniel was only *one* man, and he would be only a speck apiece for all those lions—just like one single bite of cake to a little boy, but when there were plenty of men, so that each lion could have one for himself, they made up their minds it was dinner-time, an' so they went to work."

Somehow this reply caused Mrs. Burton to forget to enforce the great moral application of the story of Daniel, and she found it convenient to make a sudden tour of inspection in the kitchen. She was growing desperately conscious that, instead of instructing and controlling the children, she had thus far done little but supply material for their active minds and bodies to employ in manners extremely distasteful to her. More than once she found her mind wavering between two extremes of the theories of government—it seemed to her that she must either be very severe, or must allow the children to naturally develop their own faculties, within reasonable bounds. At the first extreme she rebelled, partly because she was not cruel by nature, as severe rulers of children always are, and partly because the children were not her own. The other extreme was equally distasteful, however. Were not children always made to mind, in well-regulated families? To be sure, in such cases they never fulfilled, in adult years, the promise of their youth, but that, of course, was their own fault—whose else could it be? Should adults—should she, whose will had never been brooked by parent or husband—ever set aside her own inclinations for the sake of a couple of unformed, unreasoning minds?

Like most other people, when in doubt, Mrs. Burton did nothing for a few hours, and succeeded thereby in entirely losing sight of her nephews from lunch-time until nearly sunset. Then, however, impelled by that instinct which is strongest in the most immature natures, the boys returned for something to eat. Though quiet, there could be no doubt about their contentment; their clothes were very dirty, and so were their faces, but out of the latter shone that indefinable something that is the easily read indication of the consciousness of rectitude and of satisfaction with the results of right-doing. They were not very communicative, even under considerable questioning, and Mr. Burton finally said, as one in a soliloquy:

"I wonder what it was?"

"What *are* you talking about, Harry?" asked Mrs. Burton.

"I am simply wondering what original and expensive experiment they've been up to now," replied the head of the household.

"None whatever," said Mrs. Burton: "I often wonder how men can be so blind. Look at their dear, pure little faces, dirty though they are; there's no more consciousness of wrong there than there could be in an angel's face."

"Just so, my dear," said Mr. Burton. "If they were oftener conscious of misdeeds they would be worse boys, but a great deal less troublesome. Come see uncle, boys—don't you want a trot on my knees?"

Both children scrambled into their uncle's arms, and Budge began to whisper very earnestly.

"Yes, I suppose so," answered Mr. Burton, in reply.

"Goody, goody, goody!" exclaimed Budge, clapping

his hands. "I'm going to give you a birthday present to-morrow, Aunt Alice."

"So am I," said Toddie.

"It's something to eat," said Budge.

"Mine too," said Toddie.

"Be careful, Budge," said Mr. Burton. "You'll let the secret out if you're not careful."

"Oh, no, I won't," said Budge. I only said 'twas something to eat. But say, Aunt Alice, how *do* bananas grow?"

"*I* know how white grapes grows," said Toddie, with brightening eyes, and a vigorous, confident shake of his curly head.

"And I know," said Mr. Burton, lifting Toddie suddenly from his knee, "that either a certain little boy is breaking to pieces and spilling badly, or something else is. What's this?" he continued, noticing a very wet spot on Toddie's apron, just under which his pocket was. "And" (here he opened Toddie's pocket gingerly and looked into it) "what is that vile muss in your pocket?"

Toddie's eyes opened in wonder, and then his countenance fell.

"'T wash only a little bunch," said he, "an' I was goin' to eat it on the way home, but I forgotted it!"

"They're white grapes, my dear," said Mr. Burton. "The boys have been robbing somebody's hot-house. Tom has not grapes in his. Where did you get these, boys?"

"Sh—h—h!" whispered Toddie, impressively. "Nobody musht never tell secrets."

"Where did you get those grapes?" demanded Mrs. Burton, hastening to the examination of the dripping dress.

Toddie burst into tears.

"I should think you *would* cry!" exclaimed Mrs. Burton, "after stealing people's fruit."

"Isn't cryin' 'bout that," sobbed Toddie. "I'ze cryin' 'caush youze a-spoilin' my s'prise for your bifeday ev'ry minute you's a-talkin'!"

"Alice, Alice," said Mr. Burton, softly. "Remember that the poor child is not old enough to have learned what stealing means."

"Then he shall learn now!" exclaimed Mrs. Burton, all of her righteous senses alert. "What do you suppose would become of you if you were to die to-night?"

"*Won't* die," sobbed Toddie. "If angels come to kill me like he did the 'Gyptians, I'll hide."

"No one could hide from the angel of the Lord," said Mrs. Burton, determined that fear should do what reason could not.

"Why, he doesn't carry no lanternzh wif him in the night-time, does he?" asked Toddie.

Mr. Burton laughed, but Mrs. Burton silenced him with a glance, and answered:

"He can see well enough to find bad little boys when he wants them."

"*Ain't* bad," screamed Toddie, "an' I won't give you the uvver grapes now," that we brought home in a flower-pot."

"Come to uncle, old boy," said Mr. Burton, taking the doleful child upon his knee again, and caressing him tenderly; "tell uncle all about it, and he'll see if you can't be set all right."

"An' not let the killey angel come catch me?" asked Toddie.

"I'll tell you, Uncle Harry," said Budge. "We was goin' to give Aunt Alice fruit for her birthday—me bananas an' Tod white grapes. We didn't know where any bananas growed, but Mr. Bushman, way off along the mountain, has got lots of lovely grapes in his green-house, 'cause we went there once with papa, and they talked 'bout grapes an' things 'most all afternoon, an' Mr. Bushman gave papa some, an' told him to come help himself whenever he wanted any. So we made up a great secret, an' we went up there this afternoon to ask him to give us some for our aunt, 'cause 'twas goin' to be her burfday But he wasn't home, and the green-house man wasn't there either; but the door was open, an' we went in an' saw the grapes, an' we made up our minds that he wouldn't care if we took some, 'cause he told papa to, so we got three or four nice bunches, and put 'em in a flower-pot with leaves in it, and each of us got a little bunch to eat ourselves; but we found lots of wild strawberries on the way back, so Tod forgot *his* grapes, I guess, but mine's safe in my stomach. An' 'twas *awful* hot an' dusty, an' I never got so tired in my life. But we wanted to make Aunt Alice happy, so we didn't care."

"An' then she said we was fiefs," sobbed Toddie; "bad old fing!"

"Never mind, Toddie," said Mrs. Burton, all her moral purpose taking flight as she kissed the tear-stained, dirty little cheeks, and carried her nephew to the dinner-table.

Toddie's meal was quickly dispatched. He seemed preoccupied, and hurried away from the table, though he was quite ready to go to bed when summoned by his aunt. Half an hour later Mr. Burton, sauntering out to the piazza to smoke, saw a large, rude cross, in red ink, on each side of the door-frame. Even men have weaknesses, and a fastidiousness about the appearance of his house was one of Mr. Burton's. He dashed up the stairs, three steps at a time, and burst into his nephews' room, exclaiming:

"Who daubed the door with ink?"

"Me," said Toddie, boldly. "I was afraid you'd forget to tell that killey angel I wasn't any fief, so I putted crosses on the door, like the Izzyrelites did, so he would go a-past. He wouldn't know the ink wasn't blood, I guess, in the night time."

Toddie suddenly found himself at peace again.

CHAPTER IV.

MRS. BURTON's birthday dawned brightly, and as it was her first natal anniversary since her marriage to a man who had no intention or ability to cease being a lover, it is not surprising that her ante-breakfast moments were too fully and happily occupied to allow her to even think of two little boys who had already impressed upon her their willingness and general ability to think for themselves. As for the young men themselves, they awoke with the lark, and with a heavy sense of responsibility also. The room of Mrs. Burton's chambermaid joined their own, and the occupant of that room having been charged by her mistress with the general care of the boys between dark and daylight, she had gradually lost that faculty for profound slumber which so notably distinguishes the domestic servant from all other human beings. She had grown accustomed to wake at the first sound in the boys' room, and on the morning of her mistress's birthday the first sound she heard was "Tod!"

No response could be heard; but a moment later the chambermaid heard:

"T—o—o—od!"

"Ah—h—h—ow!" drawled a voice, not so sleepily but it could sound aggrieved.

"Wake up, dear old Toddie-budder—it's Aunt Alice's birthday now."

"Needn't bweak my earzh open, if *'tis*," whined Toddie.

"I only holloed in *one* ear, Tod," remonstrated Budge, "an' you ought to love dear Aunt Alice enough to have *that* hurt a little rather than not wake up."

A series of groans, snarls, whines, grunts, snorts, and remonstrances semi-articulate were heard, and at length some complicated wriggles and convulsed kicks were made manifest to the listening ear, and then Budge said:

"*That's* right; now let's get up an' get ready. Say; do you know that we didn't think anything about having some music? Don't you remember how papa played the piano last mamma's birthday when she came down stairs, an' how happy it made her, an' we danced around?"

"Aw wight," said Toddie. "Let's."

"*Tell* you what," said Budge, "let's *both* bang the piano, like mamma an' Aunt Alice does together sometimes."

"Oh, yesh!" exclaimed Toddie. "We can make some awful *big* bangsh before she can get down to tell us to don't."

Then there was heard a scurrying of light feet as the boys picked up their various articles of clothing from the corners, chairs, bureau, table, etc., where they had been tossed the night before. The chambermaid hurried to their assistance, and both boys were soon dressed. A plate containing bananas, and another with the hard-earned grapes, were on the bureau, and the boys took them and tiptoed down the stair and into the drawing-room.

"Gwacious!" said Toddie, as he placed his plate on the sideboard, "maybe the gwapes an' buttonanoes has got sour. I guesh we'd better try 'em, like mamma does the milk on hot morningsh when the baddy milkman don't come time enough," and Toddie suited the action to the word by plucking from a cluster the handsomest grape in sight. "I *fink*," said he, smacking his lips with the suspicious air of a professional wine-taster; "I fink they *is* gettin' sour."

"Let's see," said Budge.

"No," said Toddie, plucking another grape with one hand while with the other he endeavored to cover his gift. "Ize did enough to do it all myself. Unless," he added, as a happy inspiration struck him, "you'll let me help see if your buttonanoes are sour."

"Then you can only have one bite," said Budge. "You must let me taste about six grapes, 'cause 'twould take that many to make one of *your* bites on a banana."

"Aw wight," said Toddie; and the boys proceeded to exchange duties, Budge taking the precaution to hold the banana himself, so that his brother should not abstractedly sample a second time, and Toddie doling out the grapes with careful count.

"They *are* a little sour," said Budge, with a wry face. "Perhaps some other bunch is better. I think we'd better try each one, don't you?"

"An' each one of the buttonanoes, too," suggested Toddie. "*That* one wazh pretty good, but maybe some of the others isn't."

The proposition was accepted, and soon each banana had its length reduced by a fourth, and the grape-clusters displayed a fine developement of wood. Then Budge seemed to realize that his present was not as sightly as it might be, for he carefully closed the skins at the ends, and turned the unbroken ends to the front as deftly as if he were a born retailer of fruit.

This done, he exclaimed: "Oh! we want our cards on 'em, else how will she know who they came from?"

"We'll be here to tell her," said Toddie.

"Huh!" said Budge; "that wouldn't make her half so happy. Don't you know how when cousin Florence gets presents of flowers, she's always happiest when she's lookin' at the card that comes with 'em?"

"Aw wight," said Toddie, hurrying into the parlor, and

returning with two cards taken haphazard from his aunt's card-receiver.

"Now, we must write 'Happy Birthday' on the backs of 'em," said Budge, exploring his pockets, and extracting a stump of a lead-pencil. "Now," continued Budge, leaning over the card, and displaying all the facial contortions of the unpracticed writer, as he laboriously printed, in large letters, speaking, as he worked, a letter at a time.

"H—A—P—P—E B—U—R—F—D—A—Happy Birthday. Now, you must hold the pencil for yours, or else it won't be so sweet—that's what mamma says."

Toddie took the pencil in his pudgy hand, and Budge guided the hand; and two juvenile heads touched each other, and swayed, and twisted, and bobbed in unison until the work was completed.

"Now, I think she ought to come," said Budge. (Breakfast-time was still more than an hour distant.) "Why, the rising-bell hasn't rung yet! Let's ring it!"

The boys fought for possession of the bell; but superior might conquered, and Budge marched up and down the hall, ringing with the enthusiasim and duration peculiar to the amateur.

"Bless me!" exclaimed Mrs. Burton, hastening to complete her toilet. "How time does fly—sometimes!"

Mr. Burton saw something in his wife's face that seemed to call for lover-like treatment; but it was not without a sense of injury that he exclaimed, immediately after, as he drew forth his watch:

"I declare! I would make an affidavit that we hadn't been awake half an hour. Ah! I forgot to wind up my watch last night."

The boys hurried into the parlor.

"I hear 'em trampin' around!" exclaimed Budge, in great excitement. "There!—the piano's shut! Isn't that *too* mean! Oh, *I'll* tell you—here's Uncle Harry's violin."

"Then whatsh *I* goin' to play on?" asked Toddie, dancing frantically about.

"Wait a minute," said Budge, dropping the violin, and hurrying to the floor above, from which he speedily returned with a comb. A bound volume of the *Portfolio* lay upon the table, and opening this, Budge tore the tissue-paper from one of the etchings and wrapped the comb in it.

"There!" said he, "you fiddle, an' I'll blow the comb. Goodness! why *don't* they come down? Oh, we forgot to put pennies under the plate, and we don't know how many years old to put 'em for."

"An' we ain't got no pennies," said Toddie.

"*I* know," said Budge, hurrying to a cabinet in a drawer of which his uncle kept the nucleus of a collection of American coinage. "This kind of pennies," Budge

"There!" said Budge, "you fiddle an' I'll blow the comb—Goodness, why *don't* they come down." (*Page* 92.)

continued, "isn't so pretty as our kind, but they're bigger, an' they'll look better on a table-cloth. Now how old do you think she is?"

"I dunno," said Toddie, going into a reverie of hopeless conjecture. "She's about as big as you an' me put togevver."

"Well," said Budge, "you're four an' I'm six, an' four an' six is ten—I guess ten'll be about the thing."

Mrs. Burton's plate was removed, and the pennies were deposited in a circle. There was some painful counting and recounting, and many disagreements, additions and subtractions. Finally, the pennies were arranged in four rows, two of three each and two of two each, and Budge counted the threes and Toddie verified the twos; and Budge was adding the four sums together, when footsteps were heard descending the stairs.

Budge hastily dropped the surplus coppers upon the four rows, replaced the plate, and seized the comb as Toddie placed the violin against his knee, as he had seen small, itinerant Italians do. A second or two later, as the host and hostess entered the dining-room, there arose a sound which caused Mrs. Burton to clap her fingers to her ears, while her husband exclaimed:

"'Scat!"

Then both boys dropped their instruments, Toddie finding the ways of his own feet seriously compromised by the strings of the violin, while both children turned happy faces toward their aunt, and shouted :

"Happy burfday !"

Mr. Burton hurried to the rescue of his darling instrument, while his wife gave each boy an appreciative kiss, and showed them a couple of grateful tears. Then her eye was caught by the fruit on the sideboard, and she read the cards aloud :

"Mrs. Frank Rommery—this is just like her effusiveness. I've never met her but once, but I suppose her bananas must atone for her lack of manners. Why, Charley Crewne ! Dear me ! What memories some men have !"

A cloud came upon Mr. Burton's brow. Charlie Crewne had been one of his rivals for Miss Mayton's hand, and Mrs. Burton was looking a trifle thoughtful, and her husband was as unreasonable as newly-made husbands are sure to be, when Mrs. Burton exclaimed :

"Some one has been picking the grapes off in the most shameful manner. Boys !"

"*Ain't* from no Rommerys an' Crewnes," said Toddie. "Theysh from me an' Budgie, an' we dzust tasted 'em to see if they'd got sour in the night."

"Where did the cards come from ?" asked Mrs. Burton.

"Out of the basket in the parlor," said Budge ; "but the back is the nice part of 'em."

Mrs. Burton's thoughtful expression and her husband's frown disappeared together as they deciphered the inscriptions made by the boys, and seated themselves at the table. Both boys wriggled vigorously until their aunt raised her plate, and then Budge exclaimed:

"A penny for each year, you know."

"Thirty-one!" exclaimed Mrs. Burton, after counting the heap. "How complimentary!"

"What doesh you do for little boys on your bifeday?" asked Toddie, after breakfast was served. "Mamma does *lots* of fings."

"Yes," said Budge, "she says she thinks people ought to get their own happy by makin' other people happy. An' mamma knows better than you, you know, 'cause she's been married longest."

Although Mrs. Burton admitted the facts, the inference seemed scarcely natural, and she said so.

"Well—a—a—a—a—*any*how," said Toddie, "mamma always has parties on her bifeday, an' we hazh all the cake we want."

"You shall be happy to-day, then," said Mrs. Burton; "for a few friends will be in to see me this afternoon, and I am going to have a nice little lunch for them, and you shall lunch with us, if you will be very good until then, and keep yourselves clean and neat."

"Aw wight," said Toddie. "Izhn't it most time now?"

"Tod's all stomach," said Budge, with some contempt. "Say, Aunt Alice, I hope you won't forget to have some fruit-cake. That's the kind *we* like best."

"You'll come home very early, Harry?" asked Mrs. Burton, ignoring her nephew's question.

"By noon, at furthest," said the gentleman. "I only want to see my morning letters, and fill any orders that may be in them."

"What are you coming so early for, Uncle Harry?" asked Budge.

"To take Aunt Alice riding, old boy," said Mr. Burton.

"Oh! just listen, Tod! Won't that be jolly? Uncle Harry's going to take us riding!"

"I said I was going to take your Aunt Alice, Budge," said Mr. Burton.

"I heard you," said Budge, "but that won't trouble us any. She always likes to talk to you better than she does to us, an' we like her to be happy. When are we going?"

Mr. Burton asked his wife, in German, whether the Lawrence-Burton assurance was not charmingly natural, and Mrs. Burton answered in the same tongue that it was, but was none the less deserving of rebuke, and that she felt it to be her duty to tone it down in her nephews. Mr. Burton wished her joy of the attempt, and asked a number of searching questions about success already attained, until Mrs. Burton was glad to see Toddie come out of a brown study and hear him say:

"I fink that placesh where the river is bwoke off izh the nicest placesh."

"What *does* the child mean?" asked his aunt.

"Don't you know where we went last year, an' you stopped us from seein' how far we could hang over, Uncle Harry?" said Budge.

"Oh—Passaic Falls," exclaimed Mr. Burton.

"Yes, that's it," said Budge.

"Old riverzh bwoke wight in two there," said Toddie, "an' a piece of it's way up in the air, an' anuvver piece izh way down in big hole in the stonesh. That'sh where I want to go widin'."

"Listen, Toddie," said Mrs. Burton. "We like to take you riding with us at most times, but *to-day* we prefer to go alone. You and Budge will stay at home—we sha'n't be gone more than two hours."

"Wantsh to go a-widin'," exclaimed Toddie.

"I know you do, dear, but you must wait until some other day," said the lady.

"But I *wantsh* to go," Toddie explained.

"And I don't want you to, so you can't," said Mrs. Burton, in a tone which would reduce any reasonable person to hopelessness. But Toddie, in spite of manifest astonishment, remarked:

"Wantsh to go a-widin'."

"*Now* the fight is on," murmured Mr. Burton to himself. Then he arose hastily from the table, and said:

"I think I'll try to catch the earlier train, my dear, as I am coming back so soon."

Mrs. Burton arose to bid her husband good-by, and was kissed with more than usual tenderness, and then held at arm's length, while manly eyes looked into her own with an expression which she found untranslatable—for two hours, at least. Mrs. Burton saw her husband fairly on his way, and then she returned to the dining-room, led Toddie into the parlor, took him upon her lap, wound her arms tenderly about him, and said:

"Now, Toddie, dear, listen carefully to what Aunt Alice tells you. There are some reasons why you boys should not go with us to-day, and Aunt Alice means just what she says when she tells you, you can't go with us. If you were to ask a hundred times it would not make the slightest bit of difference. You cannot go, and you must stop thinking about it."

Toddie listened intelligently from beginning to end, and replied:

"But I *wantsh* to go."

"And you cant't That ends the matter."

"No, it don't," said Toddie—"not a single bittie. I wantsh to go badder than ever."

"But you are not going."

"I wantsh to go *so* baddy," said Toddie, beginning to cry

"I suppose you do, and auntie is very sorry for you," said Mrs. Burton, kindly: "but that does not alter the case. When grown people say 'No!' little boys must understand that they mean it."

"But what I wantsh izh to go a-widin' wif you," said Toddie.

"And what *I* want is, that you shall stay at home; so you must," said Mrs. Burton. "Let us have no more talk about it now. Shouldn't you like to go into the garden and pick some strawberries all for yourself?"

"No; I'd like to go widin'."

"Toddie," said Mrs. Burton, "don't let me hear one more word about riding."

"Well, I want to go."

"Toddie, I will certainly have to punish you if you say any more on this subject, and that will make me very unhappy. You don't want to make auntie unhappy on her birthday, do you?"

"No; but I *do* want to go a-widin'."

"Listen, Toddie," said Mrs. Burton, with an imperious stamp of her foot, and a sudden loss of her entire stock of patience. "If you say one more word about that trip, I shall lock you up in the attic chamber, where you were day before yesterday, and Budge shall not be with you."

Toddie gave vent to a perfect torrent of tears, and screamed:

"A—h—h—h! I don't want to be locked up, an' I *do* want to go a-widin'!"

Toddie suddenly found himself clasped tightly in his aunt's arm, in which position he kicked, pushed, screamed and roared, during the passage of two flights of stairs. The moment of his final incarceration was marked by a piercing shriek which escaped from the attic-window, causing the dog Terry to retire precipitately from a pleasant lounging-place on the well-curb, and making a passing farmer to rein up his horses, and maintain a listening position for the space of five minutes. Meanwhile Mrs. Burton descended to the parlor, more flushed, untidy, and angry than any one had ever before seen her. She soon encountered the gaze of her nephew Budge, and it was so full of solemnity, inquiry, and reproach that Mrs. Burton's anger departed in an instant.

"How would *you* like to be carried up-stairs screamin' an' put in a lonely room, just 'cause you wanted to go riding?" asked Budge.

Mrs. Burton was unable to imagine herself in any such position, but replied:

"I should never be so foolish as to keep on wanting what I knew I could not have."

"Why!" exclaimed Budge. "Are grown folks as smart as all that?"

Mrs. Burton's conscience smote her not overlightly, and she hastened to change the subject, and to devote herself assiduously to Budge, as if to atone for some injury which she might have done to his brother. An occasional howl which fell from the attic-window increased her zeal for Budge's comfort. Under each one, however, her resolution grew weaker, and finally, with a hypocritical excuse to Budge, Mrs. Burton hurried up to the door of Toddie's prison, and said through the keyhole:

"Toddie?"

"What?" said Toddie.

"Will you be a good boy, now!"

"Yesh, if you'll take me a-widin'."

Mrs. Burton turned abruptly away, and simply flew down the stairs. Budge, who awaited her at the foot, instinctively stood aside, and exclaimed:

"My! I thought you was goin' to tumble! Why didn't you bring him down?"

"Bring who?" asked Mrs. Burton, indignantly.

"Oh, *I* know what you went up-stairs for," said Budge. Your eyes told me all about it."

"You're certainly a rather inconvenient companion," said Mrs. Burton, averting her face, "and I want you to run home and ask how your mamma and baby-sister are. Don't stay long; remember that lunch will be earlier than usual to-day."

Away went Budge, and Mrs Burton devoted herself to thought and self-questioning. Unquestioning obedience had been her own duty since first she could remember, yet she was certain that her will was as strong as Toddie's. If she had been always able to obey, certainly the unhappy little boy in the attic was equally capable—why should he not do it? Perhaps, she admitted to herself, she had inherited a faculty in this directon, and perhaps—yes, certainly, Toddie had done nothing of the sort. How was she to overcome the defect in his disposition; or was she to do it at all! Was it not something with which no one temporarily having a child in charge should interfere? As she pondered, an occasional scream from Toddie helped to unbend the severity of her principles, but suddenly her eye rested upon a picture of her husband, and she seemed to see in one of the eyes a quizzical expression. All her determination came back in an instant with heavy reinforcements, and Budge came back a few moments later. His bulletins from home, and his stores of experiences *en route* consumed but a few moments, and then Mrs. Burton proceeded to dress for her ride. To exclude Toddie's screams she closed her door tightly, but Toddie's voice was one with which all timber seemed in sympathy, and it pierced door and window apparently without effort. Gradually, however, it seemed to cease, and with the growing infrequency of his howls and the increasing feebleness of their utterance, Mrs. Burton's spirits revived. Dressing leisurely, she ascended Toddie's prison to receive his declaration of penitence and to accord a gracious pardon. She knocked softly at the door, and said:

"Toddie?"

There was no response, so Mrs. Burton knocked and called with more energy than before, but without reply. A terrible fear occurred to her; she had heard of children who screamed themselves to death when angry. Hastily she opened the door, and saw Toddy, tear-stained and dirty, lying on the floor. She stooped over him to be sure that he still breathed, and then the expression on his sweetly parted lips was such, that she could not help kissing it. Then she raised the sleeping, pathetic, desolate little figure softly in her arms, and the little head dropped upon her shoulder and nestled close to her neck, and one little arm stole softly around her throat, and a soft voice murmured:

"I wantsh to go a-widin'."

And just then Mr. Burton entered, and, with a most exasperating affectation of ingenuousness and uncertainty, asked:

"Did you conquer his will, my dear?"

His wife annihilated him with a look, and led the way to the dining-room; meanwhile, Toddy awoke, straightened himself, rubbed his eyes, recognized his uncle, and exclaimed:

"Uncle Harry, does you know where we's goin' this afternoon? We's goin' a-widin'."

And Mr. Burton hid in his napkin all of his face that was below his eyes, and his wife wished that his eyes might have been hidden, too, for never in her life had she been so averse to having her own eyes looked into.

The extreme saintliness of both boys during the afternoon's ride, took the sting out of Mrs. Burton's defeat. They gabbled to each other about flowers, and leaves, and birds, and they assumed ownership of a few summer clouds that were visible, and made sundry exchanges of them with each other. When the dog Terry, who had surreptitiously followed the carriage and grown weary, was taken in by his master, they even allowed him to lie at their feet without kicking, pinching his ears, or pulling his tail.

As for Mrs. Burton, no right-minded husband could willfully torment his wife upon her birthday, so she soon forgot the humiliation of the morning, and came home with superb spirits and matchless complexion for the little party. Her guests soon began to arrive, and after the company was assembled, Mrs. Burton's chambermaid ushered in Budge and Toddie, each in spotless attire, and the dog Terry ushered himself in, and Toddie saw him and made haste to interview him, and the two got inextricably mixed about the legs of a light *jardinière*, and it came down with a crash, and then the two were sent into disgrace, which suited them exactly, although there was a difference between them, as to whether the dog Terry should seek and enjoy the seclusion upon which his heart was evidently intent.

Then Budge retired with a face full of fatherly solicitude, and Mrs. Burton was enabled to devote herself to the friends to whom she had not previously been able to address a single uninterrupted sentence.

Mrs. Burton occasionally suggested to her husband, that it might be well to see where the boys were and what they were doing, but that gentleman had seldom before found himself the only man among a dozen comely and intelligent ladies, and he was too conscious of the rarity of such experiences to trouble himself about a couple of people who had unlimited ability to keep themselves out of trouble; so the boys were undisturbed during two hours. A sudden summer shower came up in the meantime, and a sentimental young lady requested the song "The Rain upon the Roof," and Mrs. Burton and her husband began to render it as a duet; but in the middle of the second stanza Mrs. Burton began to cough, and Mr. Burton sniffed the air apprehensively, while several of the ladies started to their feet, while others turned pale. The air of the room was evidently filling with smoke.

"There can't be any danger, ladies," said Mrs. Burton. "You all know what the American domestic servant is. I suppose our cook, with her delicate sense of the appropriate, is re-lighting her fire, and has the kitchen doors wide open, so that all the smoke may escape through the house instead of the chimney. I'll go and stop it."

The mere mention of servants had its usual effect; the ladies began at once that animated conversation which this subject has always inspired, and which it will probably continue to inspire until all housekeepers gather in that happy land, one of whose charms it is that the American kitchen is undiscernible within its borders, and the redeemed domestic may stand before her mistress without needing a scolding But one nervous young lady, whose agitation was being manifested by her feet alone, happened to touch with the toe of her boot the turn-screw of the hot-air register. Instantly she sprang back and uttered a piercing scream, while from the register, there arose a thick column of smoke.

"Fire!" screamed one lady.

"Water!" shrieked another.

"Oh!" shouted several in chorus.

Some ran up-stairs, others into the rainy street, the nervous young lady fainted, a business-like young matron, who had for years been maturing plans of operation in case of fire, hastily swept into a table-cover a dozen books in special morocco bindings, and hurried through the rain with them to a house several hundred feet away, while the faithful dog Terry, scenting the trouble afar off, hurried home and did his duty to the best of his ability by barking and snapping furiously at every one, and galloping frantically through the house, leaving his mark upon almost every square yard of the carpet Meanwhile Mr. Burton hurried up-stairs coatless, with disarranged hair, dirty hands, smirched face, and assured the ladies that there was no danger, while Budge and Toddie, the former deadly pale, and the latter almost apoplectic in color, sneaked up to their own chamber.

The company dispersed; ladies who had expected carriages did not wait for them, but struggled to the extreme verge of politeness for the use of such umbrellas and waterproof cloaks as Mrs. Burton could supply. Fifteen minutes later the only occupant of the parlor was the dog Terry, who lay, with alert head, in the center of a large Turkish chair. Mrs. Burton, tenderly supported by her husband, descended the stair, and contemplated with tightly-compressed lips and blazing eyes the disorder of her desolated parlor. When, however, she reached the dining-room and beheld the exquisitely-set lunch-table, to the arrangement of which she had devoted hours of thought in preceding days and weeks, she burst into a flood of tears.

"I'll tell you how it was," remarked Budge, who appeared suddenly and without invitation, and whose consciousness of good intention made him as adamant before the indignant frowns of his uncle and aunt. "*I* always think bonfires is the nicest things about celebrations, an' Tod an' me have been carrying sticks for two days to make a big bonfire in the back-yard to-day. But then it rained, an' rainy sticks won't burn—I *guess* we found that out last Thanksgivin' Day. So we thought we'd make one in the cellar, 'cause the top is all tin, an' the bottom's all dirt, an' it can't rain in there at all An' we got lots of newspapers and kindlin' wood, an' put some kerosene on it, an' it blazed up beautiful, an' we was just comin' up to ask you all down to look at it, when in came Uncle Harry, an' banged me against the wall an' Tod into the coal-heap, an' threw a mean old dirty carpet on top of it, an' wetted it all over"

"Little boysh never *can* do anyfing nysh wivout bein' made to don't," said Toddie. "Dzust see what an awful big splinter I got in my hand when I was froin' wood on the fire! I didn't cry a *bit* about it then, 'cause I fought I was makin' uvver folks happy, like the Lord wants little boysh to. But they didn' *get* happy, so now I *am* goin' to cry 'bout the splinter!"

And Toddie raised a howl which was as much superior to his usual cry as things made to order generally are over the ordinary supply.

"We had a torchlight procession, too," said Budge. "We had to have it in the attic, but it wasn't very nice. There wasn't any trees up there for the light to dance around on, like it does on 'lection-day nights. So we just stopped, an' would have felt real doleful if we hadn't thought of the bonfire."

"Where did you leave the torches?" asked Mr. Burton, springing from his chair, and lifting his wife to her feet at the same time.

"I—I dunno," said Budge, after a moment of thought

"Froed 'em in a closet where the rags is, so's not to dyty the nice floor wif 'em," said Toddie.

Mr. Burton hurried up-stairs and extinguished a smoldering heap of rags, while his wife, truer to herself than she imagined she was, drew Budge to her, and said, kindly:

"*Wanting* to make people happy, and *doing* it are two very different things, Budge."

"Yes, I should think they were," said Budge, with an emphasis which explained much that was left unsaid.

"Little boysh is goosies for tryin' to make big folksh happy at all," said Toddie, beginning again to cry.

"Oh, no, they're not, dear," said Mrs. Burton, taking the sorrowful child into her lap. "But they don't always understand how best to do it, so they ought to ask big folks before they begin."

"Then there wouldn't be no s'prises," complained Toddie. "Say; izh we goin' to eat all this supper?"

"I suppose so, if we can," sighed Mrs. Burton.

"I *guesh* we can—Budgie an' me," said Toddie. "An' *won't* we be glad all them wimmens wented away!"

That evening, after the boys had retired, Mrs. Burton seemed a little uneasy of mind, and at length she said to her husband:

"I feel guilty at never having directed the boys' devotions since they have been here, and I know no better time than the present in which to begin."

Mr. Burton's eyes followed his wife reverently as she left the room. The service she proposed to render the children she had sometimes performed for himself, with results for which he could not be grateful enough, and yet it was not with unalloyed anticipation that he softly followed her up the stair. Mrs. Burton went into the chamber and found the boys playing battering-ram, each with a pillow in front of him.

"Children," said she, "have you said your prayers?"

"No," said Budge; "somebody's got to be knocked down first. *Then* we will."

A sudden tumble by Toddie was the signal for devotional exercises, and both boys knelt beside the bed.

"Now, darlings," said Mrs. Burton, "you have made some sad mistakes to-day, and they should teach you that, even when you want most to do right, you need to be helped by somebody better. Don't you think so?"

"*I* do," said Budge. "Lots."

"*I* don't," said Toddie. "More help I getsh, the worse fings is. Guesh I'll do fings all alone affer thish."

"I know what to say to the Lord to-night, Aunt Alice," said Budge.

"*Dear* little boy," said Mrs. Burton, "go on."

"Dear Lord," said Budge, "we *do* have the *awfullest* times when we try to make other folks happy. *Do*, please, Lord—please teach big folks how hard little folks have to think before they do things for 'em. An' make 'em understand little folks *every* way better than they do, so that they don't make little folks unhappy when little folks try to make big folks feel jolly. Make big folks have to think as hard as little folks do, for Christ's sake—Amen! Oh, yes, an' bless dear mamma an' the sweet little sister baby. How's that, Aunt Alice?"

Mrs. Burton did not reply, and Budge, on turning, saw only her departing figure, while Toddie remarked:

"Now it's *my* tyne (turn). Dear Lord, when I getsh to be a little boy anzel up in hebben, don't let growed-up anzels come along whenever I'm doin' anyfing nice for 'em, an' say '*don't*' or tumble me down in heaps of nashty old black coal. *There!* Amen!"

CHAPTER V.

It was with a sneaking sense of relief that Mrs. Burton awoke on the following morning, and realized that the day was Sunday. Even school-teachers have two days of rest in every seven, thought Mrs. Burton to herself, and no one doubts that they deserve them. How much more deserving of rest and relief, then, must be the volunteer teacher who, not for a few hours only, but from dawn to twilight, has charge of two children whose capacity for both learning and mischief surely equals any schoolful of boys? The realization that she was attempting, for a few days only, that which mothers everywhere were doing without hope of rest excepting in heaven, made Mrs. Burton feel more humble and worthless than she had ever done in her life before, but it did not banish her wish to turn the children over to the care of their uncle for the day. If Mrs. Burton had been honest with herself, she would have admitted that the principal cause of her anxiety for relief was her unwillingness to have her husband witness the failures, which she had come to believe were to be her daily lot while trying to train her nephews. Thoughts of a Sunday excursion, from participation in which she should in some way excuse herself; of volunteering to relieve her sister-in-law's nurse during the day, and thus leaving her husband in charge of the house and the children; of making that visit to her mother which is always in order with the newly made wife—all these, and other devices not so practicable, came before Mrs. Burton's mind's eye for comparison, but they all and together took sudden wing when Mr. Burton awoke and complained of a raging toothache Truly pitiful and sympathetic as Mrs. Burton was, she exhibited remarkable resignation in the face of the thought that her husband would probably need to remain in his room all day, and that it would be absolutely necessary to keep the children out of his sight and hearing. Then he could find nothing to criticise; she might fail as frequently as she probably would, but he would know only of her successes.

A light knock was heard at Mrs. Burton's door, and then, without waiting for invitation, there came in two fresh, rosy faces, two heads of disarranged hair, and two long white nightgowns, and the occupant of the longer gown exclaimed:

"Say, Uncle Harry, do you know it's Sunday? What are you going to do about it? We always have lots done for us Sundays, 'cause it's the only day papa's home."

"Yes, I—think I've heard—something of the kind—before," mumbled Mr Burton, with difficulty, between the fingers which covered his aching incisor.

"Oh—h," exclaimed Toddie, "I b'lieve he' goin' to play bear! Come on, Budgie, we's got to be dogs." And Toddie buried his face in the bed-covering and succeeded in fastening his teeth in his uncle's calf A howl from the sufferer did not frighten off the amateur dog, and he was finally dislodged only by being clutched by the throat by his victim.

"*That* izhn't the way to play bear," complained Toddie; "you ought to keep on a-howlin' an' let me keep on a bitin', an' then you give me pennies to stop—that's the way papa does."

"*Can* you see how Tom Lawrence can be so idiotic?" asked Mrs. Burton.

"I suppose I could," replied the gentleman, "if I hadn't such a toothache."

"You poor old fellow!" said Mrs. Burton, tenderly Then she turned to her nephews, and exclaimed: "Now, boys, listen to me! Uncle Harry is very sick to-day—he has a dreadful toothache, and every bother and noise will make it worse. You must both keep away from his room, and be as quiet as possible wherever you may be in the house. Even the sound of people talking is very annoying to a person with the toothache."

"Then you's a baddy woman to stay in here an' keep a-talkin' all the whole time," said Toddie, "when it makes poor old Uncle Harry supper so. G'way!"

Mrs. Burton's lord and master was not in too much pain to shake considerably with silent laughter over this unexpected rebuke, and the lady herself was too thoroughly startled to devise an appropriate reply, so the boys amused themselves by a general exploration of the chamber, not omitting even the pockets of their uncle's clothing. This work completed, to the full extent of their ability, the boys demanded breakfast.

"Breakfast won't be ready until eight o'clock," said Mrs. Burton, "and it is now only six. If you, little boys, don't want to feel dreadfully hungry, you had better go back to bed, and lie as quiet as possible."

"Is that the way not to be hungry?" asked Toddie, with the wide-open eyes which always accompany the receptive mind.

"Certainly," said Mrs. Burton. "If you run about, you agitate your stomachs, and that makes them restless and so you feel hungry."

"Gwacious!" said Toddie. "What lots of fings little boys has got to lyne (learn), hazn't they! Come on, Budgie—let's go put our tummuks to bed, an' keep 'em from gettin' ajjerytated."

"All right," said Budge. "But say, Aunt Alice, don't

you s'pose our stomachs would be sleepier an' not so restless if there was some crackers or bread an' butter in 'em?"

"There's no one down-stairs to get you any," said Mrs. Burton.

"Oh," said Budge, "*we* can find 'em We know where everything is in the pantries and store-room."

"*I* wish *I* were so smart," sighed Mrs. Burton. "Go along—get what you want—but don't come back to this room again. And don't let me find anything in disorder down-stairs, or I shall never trust you in my kitchen again"

Away flew the children, but their disappearance only made room for a new torment, for Mr. Burton stopped in the middle of the operation of shaving himself, and remarked:

"I've been longing for Sunday to come, for your sake, my dear. The boys, as you have frequently observed, have very strange notions about holy things; but they are also, by nature, quite religious and spiritually minded *You* are not only this latter, but you are free from strange doctrines and the traditions of men. The mystical influences of the day will make themselves felt upon those innocent little hearts, and you will have the opportunity to correct wrong teachings and instill new sentiments and truths."

Mr. Burton's voice had grown a little shaky as he reached the close of this neat and reverential speech, so that his wife scrutinized his face closely to see if there might not be a laugh somewhere about it. A friendly coating of lather protected one cheek, however, and the troublesome tooth had distorted the shape of the other, so Mrs. Burton was compelled to accept the mingled ascription of praise and responsibility, which she did with a sinking heart.

"I'll take care of them while you're at church, my dear," said Mr. Burton; "they're always saintly with sick people."

Mrs. Burton breathed a sigh of relief. She determined that she would extemporize a special "Children's service" immediately after breakfast, and impress her nephews as fully as possible with the spirit of the day, then if her husband would but continue the good work thus begun, it would be impossible for the boys to fall from grace in the few hours which remained between dinner-time and darkness. Full of her project, she forgot that she had allowed her chambermaid to go to early mass and that she had promised to see that the children were dressed for breakfast, Mrs. Burton, at the breakfast-table, noticed that her nephews did not respond with their usual alacrity to the call of the bell. Recalling her forgotten duty, she hurried to the boys' chamber, and found them already enjoying a repast which was remarkable at least for variety. On a small table, drawn to the side of the bed, was a pie, a bowl of pickles, a dish of honey in the comb, and a small paper package of cinnamon bark, and, with spoons, knives and forks and fingers, the boys were helping themselves alternately to these delicacies Seeing his aunt, Toddie looked rather guilty, but Budge displayed the smile of the fully justified, and remarked :

"Now, you know what kind of meals little boys like, Aunt Alice. I hope you won't forget it while we're here."

"What do you mean!" exclaimed Mrs. Burton, sternly, "by bringing such things up-stairs?"

"Why," said Budge, "you told us to get what we wanted an' we supposed you told the troof."

"An' I ain't azh hungry azh I wazh," remarked Toddie, "but my tummuk feels as if it growed big and got little again, every minute or two, an' it hurts I wishes we could put tummuks away when we get done usin' 'em, like we do hats an' overshoes."

To sweep the remains of the unique morning lunch into a heap and away from her nephews, was a work which occupied but a second or two of Mrs. Burton's time; this done, two little boys found themselves robed more rapidly than they had ever before been. Arrived at the breakfast-table, they eyed with withering contempt an irreproachable

"An' I aint azh hungry azh I wazh," remarked Toddie, "but my tummuk feels as if it growed big and got little again every minute or two an' it hurts. I wish we could put tummuks away when we get done usin' 'em, like we do hats an' overshoes." (*Page* 118.)

cutlet some crisp brown potatoes of wafer-like thinness, and a heap of rolls almost as light as snowflakes.

"*We* don't want none of *this* kind of breakfast," said Budge.

"Of coursh we don't," said Toddie; "when we's so awful full of uvver fings. *I* don't know where I'zhe goin' to put my dinner when it comes time to eat it."

"Don't fret about *that*, Tod," said Budge. "Don't you know papa says that the Bible says something that means 'don't worry till you have to'?"

Mrs. Burton raised her eyebrows with horror not unmixed with inquiry, and her husband hastened to give Budge's sentiment its proper Biblical wording. "Sufficient unto the day is the evil thereof." Mrs. Burton's wonder was allayed by the explanation, although her horror was not, and she made haste to say:

"Boys, we will have a little Sunday-school, all by ourselves, in the parlor, immediately after breakfast."

"Hooray!" shouted Budge. "An' will you give us tickets, an' pass around a box for pennies, just like they do in *big* Sunday-schools?"

"I—suppose so," said Mrs. Burton, who had not previously thought of these special attractions of the successful Sunday-school.

"Let's go right in, Tod," said Budge, "'cause the dog's in there. I saw him as I came down, and I shut all the doors so he couldn't get out. We can have some fun with him 'fore Sunday-school begins."

Both boys started for the parlor-door, and, guided by that marvelous instinct with which Providence arms the few against the many, and the weak against the strong, the dog Terry also approached the door from the inside. As the door opened there was heard a convulsive howl, and a general tumbling of small boys, while at almost the same instant the dog Terry flew into the dining-room and hid himself in the folds of his mistress's morning-robe. Two or three minutes later Budge entered the dining-room with a very rueful countenance, and remarked:

"I guess we need that Sunday-school pretty quick, Aunt Alice. The dog don't want to play with us, and we ought to be comforted some way."

"They're grown people, all over again," remarked Mr. Burton, with a laugh.

"What do you mean?" demanded Mrs. Burton.

"Only this—that when their own devices fail, they're in a hurry for the consolations of religion," said Mr. Burton. "May I visit the Sunday-school?"

"I suppose I can't keep you away," sighed Mrs. Burton, leading the way to the parlor. "Boys," said she, greeting her nephews, "first, we'll sing a little hymn; what shall it be?"

"Ole Uncle Ned," said Toddie, promptly.

"Oh, that's not a Sunday song," said Mrs. Burton.

"*I* fink tizh," said Toddie, "'cause it sayzh, free or four timezh, 'He's gone where de good niggers go,' an' that's *hebben*, you know; so it's a Sunday song."

"*I* think 'Glory, glory, hallelujah!' is nicer," said Budge, "an' I know *that's* a Sunday song, 'cause I've heard it in church."

"Aw wight," said Toddie; and he immediately started the old air himself, with the words, "There liezh the whisky-bottle, empty on the sheff," but was suddenly brought to order by a shake from his aunt, while his uncle danced about the front parlor in an ecstasy not directly traceable to toothache.

"That's not a Sunday song either, Toddie" said Mrs. Burton. "The words are real rowdyish. Where did you learn them?"

"'Round the corner from our housh," said Toddie, "an' you can sing you ole songs yourseff, if you don't like mine."

Mrs. Burton went to the piano, rambled among chords for a few seconds, and finally recalled a Sunday-school air in which Toddie joined as angelically as if his own musical taste had never been impugned.

"Now, I guess we'd better take up the collection before any little boys lose their pennies," said Budge, hurrying to the dining-room, and returning with a strawberry-box which seemed to have been specially provided for the occasion; this he passed gravely before Toddie, and Toddie held his hand over it as carefully as if he were depositing hundreds, and then Toddie took the box and passed it before Budge, who made the same dumb show, after which Budge retook the box, shook it, listened, remarked, "It don't rattle—I guess it's all paper-money, to-day," placed it upon the mantel, reseated himself, and remarked:

"*Now* bring on your lesson."

Mrs. Burton opened her Bible with a sense of utter helplessness. With the natural instinct of a person given to thoroughness, she opened at the beginning of the book, but she speedily closed it again—the first chapter of Genesis had suggested many a puzzling question even to her own orthodox mind. Turning the leaves rapidly, passing, for conscience' sake, the record of many a battle, the details of which would have delighted the boys, and hurrying by the prophecies as records not for the minds of children, she at last reached the New Testament, and the ever-new story of the only boy who ever was all that his parents and relatives could wish him to be.

"The lesson will be about Jesus," said Mrs. Burton.

"Little-boy Jesus or big-man Jesus," asked Toddie.

"A—a—both," replied the teacher, in some confusion.

"Aw wight," said Toddie. "G'won."

"There was once a time when all the world was in

trouble, without knowing exactly why," said Mrs Burton; "but the Lord understood it, for He understands everything."

"Does He know how it feels to be a little boy," asked Toddie, "an' be sent to bed when he don't want to go?"

"And He determined to comfort the world, as He always does when the world finds out it can't comfort itself," continued Mrs. Burton, entirely ignoring her nephew's questions.

"But wasn't there lotsh of little boyzh then?" asked Toddie, "an' didn't they need to be comforted as well as big folks?"

"I suppose so," said Mrs. Burton. "But He knew that if He comforted grown people, they would make the children happy."

"I wiss He'd comfort you an' Uncle Harry evry mornin', then," said Toddie. "G'won."

"So He sent His own Son—His only Son—down to the world to be a dear little baby."

"*I* should think He'd have made Him a *sister* baby," said Budge, "if He'd wanted to make everybody happy."

"He knew best," said Mrs. Burton. "And while smart people everywhere were wondering what would or could happen to quiet the restless heart of people——"

"Izh restless hearts like restless tummuks?" interrupted Toddie. "Kind o' lumpy and wabbley?"

"I suppose so," said Mrs. Burton.

"Poor folks," said Toddie, clasping his hands over his waistband: "I'zhe sorry for 'em."

"While smart folks were trying to think out what should be done," continued Mrs. Burton, "some simple shepherds, who used to sit around at night under the moon and stars, and wonder about things which they could not understand, saw a wonderfully bright star up in the sky."

"Was it one of the twinkle-twinkle kind, or one of the stand-still kind?" asked Toddie.

"I don't know," said Mrs. Burton, after a moment's reflection. "Why do you ask?"

"'Cauzh," said Toddie, "I know what 'twazh there for, an' it ought to have twinkled, 'cauzh twinkley starsh bob open an' shut that way 'cauzh they're laughin' and can't keep still, an' I know *I'd* have laughed if I'd been a star an' was goin' to make a lot of folks so awful happy. G'won."

"Then," said Mrs. Burton, looking alternately and frequently at the two accounts of the Advent, "they suddenly saw an angel, and the shepherds were afraid."

"Should fink they *would* be," said Toddie. "Everybody gets afraid when they see good people around. I 'spec' they thought the angel would say 'don't!' in about a minute."

"But the angel told them not to be afraid," said Mrs.

Burton, "for he had come to bring good news. There was to be a dear little baby born at Bethlehem, and He would make everybody happy."

"*Wouldn't* it be nice if that angel would come an' do it all over again?" said Budge. "Only he ought to pick out little boys instead of sheep fellows. *I* wouldn't be afraid of an angel."

"Neiver would I," said Toddie, "but I'd dzust go round behind him an' see how his wings was fastened on."

"Then a great many other angels came," said Mrs. Burton, "and they all sang and sang together. The poor shepherds didn't know what to make of it, but after the singing was over, they all started for Bethlehem to see that wonderful baby."

"Just like the other day we went to see the sister-baby."

"Yes," said Mrs. Burton; "but instead of finding Him in a pleasant home and a nice room, with careful friends and nurses around him, He was in a manger out in a stable."

"That was 'cause he was so smart that He could do just as He wanted to, an' be just where He liked," said Budge, "an' He was a little boy, an' little boys always like stables better than houses—I wish I could live in a stable always an' for ever."

"So do I," said Toddie, "an' sleep in mangers, 'cauzh then the horses would kick anybody that made me put on clean clothezh when I didn't want to. They gaveded him presentsh, didn't they?"

"Yes," said Mrs. Burton; "gold, frankincense, and myrrh."

"Why didn't they gave him rattles and squealeyballs, like folks did budder Phillie when *he* was a baby," asked Toddie.

"Because, Toddie," said Mrs. Burton, glad of an opportunity to get the sentiment of the story into her own hands, from which it had departed very early in the course of the lesson—"because He was no common baby, like other children. He was the Lord."

"What! The Lord once a little baby?" exclaimed Toddie.

"Yes," replied Mrs. Burton, shuddering to realize that Toddie had not before been taught of the nature of the Holy Trinity.

"An' played around like uvver little boysh?" continued Toddie.

"I—I—suppose so," said Mrs. Burton, fearing lest in trying to instill reverence into her nephews, she herself might prove irreverent.

"Did somebody say 'Don't' at *Him* every time he did anyfing?" continued Toddie.

"N—n—n—o? I imagine not," said Mrs. Burton, "because he was always good."

"*That* don't make no diffwelence," said Toddie. "The better a little boy triesh to be, the more folks says 'Don't' to him. So I guesh nobody had any time to say anyfing elsh at all to Jesus."

"What did He do next?" asked Budge, as deeply interested as if he had not heard the same story many times before.

"He grew strong in body and spirit," said Mrs. Burton, "and everybody loved him; but before He had time to do all that, an angel came and frightened His papa in a dream, and told him that the king of that country would kill little Jesus if he could find Him. So Joseph, the papa of Jesus, and Mary, His mamma, got up in the middle of the night, and started off to Egypt."

"Seems to me that Egypt was 'bout as bad in those days as Europe is now," remarked Budge. "Whenever papa tells about anybody that nobody can find, he says, 'Gone to Europe, I s'pose.' What did they do when they got there?"

"I don't know," said Mrs. Burton, musing. "I suppose the papa worked hard for money to buy good food and comfortable resting-places for his wife and baby; and I suppose the mamma walked about the fields, and picked pretty flowers for her baby to play with; and I suppose the baby cooed when His mamma gave them to Him, and laughed and danced and played, and then got tired, and came and hid His little face in His mamma's lap, and was taken into her arms and held ever so tight, and fell asleep, and that His mother looked into His face as if she would look through it, while she tried to find out what her baby would be and do when He grew up, and whether He would be taken away from *her*, while it seemed as if she couldn't live at all without having Him very closely pressed to her breast and——"

Mrs. Burton's voice grew a little shaky, and, finally, failed her entirely. Budge came in front of her, scrutinized her intently, but with great sympathy, also, and, finally, leaned his elbows on her knees, dropped his face into his own hands, looked up into her face, and remarked:

"Why, Aunt Alice, she was just like *my* mamma, wasn't she? An' I think *you* are just like both of 'em."

Mrs. Burton took Budge hastily into her arms, covered his face with kisses, and totally destroyed another chance of explaining the difference between the earthly and the heavenly to her pupils, while Toddie eyed the couple with evident disfavor, and remarked:

"*I* fink 'twould be nicer if you'd see if dinner was bein' got ready, instead of stoppin' tellin' stories an' beginnin' to hug Budgie. My tummuk's all gotted little again."

Mrs. Burton came back to the world of to-day from that of history, though not without a sigh, while the dog

Terry, who had divined the peaceful nature of the occasion so far as to feel justified in reclining beneath his mistress's chair, now contracted himself into the smallest possible space, slunk out of the doorway, and took a lively quickstep in the direction of the shrubbery. Toddie had seen him, however, and told the news to Budge, and both boys were soon in pursuit, noticing which the dog Terry speedily betook himself to that distant retirement which the dog who has experience in small boys knows so well how to discover and maintain

As the morning wore on, the boys grew restless, fought, drummed on the piano, snarled when that instrument was closed, meddled with everything that was within reach, and finally grew so troublesome that their aunt soon felt that to lose was cheaper than to save, so she left the house to the children, and sought the side of the lounge upon which her afflicted husband reclined. The divining sense of childhood soon found her out, however, and Budge remarked :

"Aunt Alice, if you're going to church, seems to me it's time you was getting ready."

"I can't go to church, Budge," sighed Mrs. Burton. "If I do, you boys will only turn the whole house upside down, and drive your poor uncle nearly crazy"

"No, we won't," said Budge. "You don't know what nice nurses we can be to sick people. Papa says nobody can even *imagine* how well we can take care of anybody until they see us do it. If you don't believe it, just leave us with Uncle Harry, an' stay home from church an' peek through the keyhole."

"Go on, Allie," said Mr. Burton. "If you want to go to church, don't be afraid to leave me. I think you *should* go—after your experience of this morning. I shouldn't think your mind could be at peace until you had joined your voice with that of the great congregation, and acknowledged yourself to be a miserable sinner."

Mrs. Burton winced, but nevertheless retired, and soon appeared dressed for church, kissed her husband and her nephews, gave many last instructions, and departed. Budge followed her with his eye until she had stepped from the piazza, and then remarked, with a sigh of relief:

"*Now* I guess we'll have what papa calls a good, old-fashioned time—we've got rid of *her*."

"Budge!" exclaimed Mr. Burton, sternly, and springing to his feet, "do you know who you are talking about? Don't you know that your Aunt Alice is my wife, and that she has saved you from many a scolding, done you many a favor, and been your best friend?"

"Oh, yes," said Budge, with at least a dozen inflections on each word, "but ev'ry day friends an' Sunday friends are kind o' different; don't you think so? *She* can't make whistles, or catch bull-frogs, or carry both of us up the mountain on her shoulders, or sing 'Roll, Jordan.'"

"And do you expect *me* to do all these things to-day?" asked Mr Burton.

"N—n—no," said Budge, "unless you should get well, an' feel just like it; but we'd like to be with somebody who *could* do 'em if he wanted to. We like ladies that's *all* ladies, but then we like men that's all men, too. Aunt Alice is a good deal like an angel, I think, and you—you *ain't*. An' we don't want to be with angels all the time until we're angels ourselves."

Mr. Burton turned over suddenly and contemplated the back of the lounge at this honest avowal of one of humanity's prominent weaknesses, while Budge continued:

"We don't want *you* to get to be an angel, so what I want to know is, how to make you well. Don't you think if I borrowed papa's horse and carriage an' took you ridin' you'd feel better? I know he'd lend 'em to me if I told him you were goin' to drive."

"And if you said you would go with me to take care of me?" suggested Mr. Burton.

"Y—e—es," said Budge, as hesitatingly as if such an idea had never occurred to him. "An' don't you think that up to the top of the Hawksnest Rock an' out to Passaic Falls would be the nicest places for a sick man to go? When you got tired of ridin' you could stop the carriage an' cut us a cane, or make us whistles, or find us pfingster apples (the seed-balls of the wild azalea), or even send us in swimming in a brook somewhere if you got tired of us."

"H'm!" grunted Mr Burton.

"An' you might take fings to eat wif you," suggested Toddie, "an' when you got real tired and felt bad, you might stop and have a little pic-nic. I fink that would be dzust the fing for a man wif the toofache. And we could help you, lotsh."

"I'll see how I feel after dinner," said Mr. Burton. "But what are you going to do for me between now and then, to make me feel better?"

"We'll tell you storiezh," said Toddie. "*Them's* what sick folks alwayzh likesh."

"Very well," said Mr. Burton. "Begin right away."

"Aw wight," said Toddie. "Do you wantsh a sad story or a jolly one."

"Anything," said Mr. Burton. "Men with the toothache can stand nearly anything. Don't draw on your imagination *too* hard."

"Don't *never* draw on no madzinasuns," said Toddie: 'I only draws on slatesh."

"Never mind; give us the story."

"Well," said Toddie, seating himself in a little rocking-chair, and fixing his eyes on the ceiling, "guesh I'll tell about AbrahammynIsaac. Onesh the Lord told a man named Abraham to go up the mountain an' chop his little boy's froat open an' burn him on a naltar, So Abraham started to go do it. An' he made his little boy Isaac, that he was going to chop and burn up, carry the kindlin' wood he was goin' to set him a-fire wiv. An' I want to know if you fink that wazh very nysh of him?"

"Well,—no," said Mr. Burton

"Tell you what," said Budge, "you don't ever catch *me* carryin' sticks up the mountain, even if my papa wants me to."

"When they got up there," said Toddie, "Abraham made a naltar an' put little Ikey on it, an' took a knife an' was goin' to chop his froat open, when a andzel came out of hebben an' said: 'Stop a-doin' that!' So Abraham stopped, an' Ikey skooted; an' Abraham saw a sheep caught in the bushes, an' he caught *him* and killed him. He wasn't goin' to climb way up a mountain to kill somebody an' not have his knife bluggy a bit. An' he burned the sheep up. An' then he went home again."

"I'll bet you Isaac's mamma never knew what his papa wanted to do with him," said Budge, "or she'd never let her little boy go away in the mornin.' Do you want to bet?"

"N—no, not on Sunday, I guess," said Mr. Burton. "Now, suppose you little boys go out of doors and play for a while, while uncle tries to get a nap."

The boys accepted the suggestion and disappeared. Half an hour later, as Mrs. Burton was walking home from church, under escort of old General Porcupine, and enduring with saintly fortitude the general's compliments upon her management of the children, there came screams of fear and anguish from the general's own grounds, which the couple were passing.

"Who can that be?" exclaimed the general, his short hairs bristling like the quills of his titular godfather. "*We* have no children."

"I—think I know the voices," gasped Mrs. Burton, turning pale.

"Bless my soul!" exclaimed the general, with an accent which showed that he was wishing the reverse of blessings upon souls less needy than his own. "You don't mean——"

"Oh, I do?" said Mrs. Burton, wringing her hands. "Do hurry!"

The general puffed and snorted up his gravel walk and toward the shrubbery, behind which was a fish-pond, from which direction the sound came. Mrs. Burton followed, in time to see her nephew Budge help his brother out of the pond, while the general tugged at a large crawfish which had fastened its claw upon Toddie's finger. The fish was game, but, with a mighty pull from the general and a superhuman shriek from Toddie, the fish's claw and body parted company, and the general, still holding the latter tightly, staggered backward, and himself fell into the pond.

"Ow—ow—ow—!" howled Toddie, clasping the skirt of his aunt's dress in a ruinous embrace, while the general floundered and snorted like a whale in dying agonies, and Budge laughed as merrily as if the whole scene had been provided especially for his entertainment. Mrs. Burton hurried her nephews away, forgetting, in her mortification, to thank the general for his service, and placing a hand over Toddie's mouth.

"It hurts!" mumbled Toddie.

"What did you touch the fish at all for?" asked Mrs. Burton.

"It was a little baby-lobster," sobbed Toddie, "an' I loves little babies—all kinds of 'em—an' I wanted to pet him. An' then I wanted to grop him."

"Why did't you do it, then?" demanded the lady.

"Cauzh he wouldn't grop," said Toddie, "he isn't all gropped yet."

True enough, the claw of the fish still hung at Toddie's finger, and Mrs. Burton spoiled a pair of four-button kids in detaching it, while Budge continued to laugh. At length, however, mirth gave place to brotherly love, and Budge tenderly remarked:

"Toddie, dear, don't you love brother Budgie?"

"Yesh," sobbed Toddie.

"Then you ought to be happy," said Budge, "for you've made *him* awful happy. If the fish hadn't caught you, the general couldn't have pulled him off, an' then he wouldn't have tumbled into the pond, an' oh, my!—*didn't* he splash bully!"

"Then *you's* got to be bited wifh a fiss," said Toddie, "an' make him tumble in again, for *me* to laugh 'bout."

"You're two naughty boys," said Mrs. Burton. "Is this the way you take care of your sick uncle?"

"*Did* take care of him," exclaimed Toddie; "told him a lovaly Bible story, an' you didn't, an' he wouldn't have had not no Sunday at all if I hadn't done it. An' we's goin' to take him widin' this afternoon."

Mrs. Burton hurried home, but it seemed to her that she had never met so many inquiring acquaintances during so short a walk. Arrived at last, she ordered her nephews to their room, and flung herself in tears beside her husband, murmuring:

"Harry!"

And Mr. Burton, having viewed the ruined dress with the eye of experience, uttered the single word:

"Boys!"

"What am I to do with them?" asked the unhappy woman.

Mr. Burton was an affectionate husband. He adored womankind, and sincerely bemoaned its special grievances; but he did not resist the temptation to recall his wife's announcement of five days before, so he whispered:

"Train them.

"I——"

Mrs. Burton's humiliation by her own lips was postponed by a heavy footfall, which by turning her face, she discovered was that of her brother-in-law, Tom Lawrence, who remarked:

"Tender confidences, eh? Well, I'm sorry I intruded. There's nothing like them if you want to be happy. But Helen's pretty well to-day, and dying to have her boys with her, and I'm even worse with a similar longing. You can't spare them, I suppose?"

The peculiar way in which Tom Lawrence's eyes danced as he awaited a reply would, at any other time, have roused all the defiance in Alice Burton's nature; but now, looking at the front of her beautiful dress, she only said:

"Why—I suppose—we *might* spare them for an hour or two!"

"You poor dear Spartan," said Tom, with genuine

sympathy, "you shall be at peace until their bedtime, anyhow."

And Mrs. Burton found occasion to re-arrange the bandage on her husband's face so as to whisper in his ear:

"Thank Heaven!"

CHAPTER VI.

THE only drawback to the perfect joy of the Burtons Sunday afternoon was the anticipation of the return of their nephews, but even this proved to be without grounds. The boys returned fast asleep, Budge on his father's arms, and Toddie's head pillowed on the shoulder of the faithful Mike; and, excepting a single sigh of "fwolic!" from Toddie, no sound was heard from either until the next morning, when, finding that the children slept later than usual Mrs. Burton went to their chamber to arouse them. She found Budge sitting up in bed rubbing his eyes with one hand, while with the other he shook his brother, and elicited some ugly grunts of remonstrance.

"Tod!" exclaimed Budge—"Tod! wake up! we ain't where we was!"

"Don't care if we isn't," said Toddie; "Izhs in—a—nicer playsh—Izhe in—big candy-shop."

"No, you ain't," said Budge, shaking vigorously, and trying to pick his brother's eyes open; "you're at Aunt

Alice's, and when you went to sleep you were at mamma's house."

"Aw—w—w—!" cried Toddie, arising slowly; "you're a hateful bad boy, Budgie; I was a-dreamin' I was in a candy-store, and gotted all my pockets full an' bofe hands full, too, an' now you's woketed me up an' my hands is all empty, an' I hazn't got any pocket-clozhezh on me at all."

"Well, *next* time you have a dream I won't wake you at all, even if you have nightmares, an' dream awful things. Say, Aunt Alice," continued Budge, "how *do* folks dream, I wonder? What makes everything go away an' be something else?"

"It is the result of indistinct impressions upon a semi-dormant brain," said Mrs. Burton.

"Oh!" said Budge.

Mrs. Burton thought she detected a note of sarcasm in her nephew's exclamation, but he was so young, and he seemed so meek of countenance, that she abandoned the suspicion. Besides, her younger nephew had been saying, "Aunt Alish—Aunt Alish—Aunt Alish—Aunt Alish—" as rapidly as he could and with an increasing volume of voice Mrs. Burton finally found time in which to say:

"What?"

"Did you say pressin' on byains made us dream fings, Aunt Alish?"

"Yes," said Mrs. Burton; "that is the——"

"Well, then," interrupted Toddie, "dzust you sit down on my head an' make that candy-shop come back again, won't you?"

"Say, Aunt Alice," said Budge, "do you know that lots of times I don't know any more than I knew before?"

"I don't understand you, Budge."

"Why, when folks tell me things—I mean, I ask them how things are, and they tell me, and then I don't know any better than I did before. Is that the way it is with grown folks?"

Mrs Burton reflected for a moment and recalled many experiences very much like that of Budge—experiences, too, in which she had forced the same impassive face that Budge wore, as she pretended to comprehend that which had been imperfectly explained; she remembered, too, how depressing had been the lack of understanding, and how strong was the sense of injury at being required to act as if her comprehension had been perfectly reached. Whether the topics had been the simple affairs of childhood, or the social, æsthetic and religious instructions of adult age, Mrs. Burton, like every one else, had been told more than she had understood, and misunderstood many things which she had been told, and blamed her friends and the world for her blunders, and for lack of apprecia- tion of the intentions to which proper and fostering training had never been applied. Was it possible that she was repeating with her nephews the blunders which others had committed while attempting to shape her own mind?

The thought threw Mrs. Burton into the profoundest depths of reverie, from which she was aroused by Budge, who asked:

"Aunt Alice, do you see the Lord?"

"No, Budge," exclaimed Mrs. Burton, with a start. "Why do you ask?"

"Why," said Budge, "you were looking so hard through the window, an' right toward where you couldn't see anything but sky; an' your eyes had such an ever-so-far look in them that I thought you *must* be lookin' straight at the Lord."

"If you sees Him," remarked Toddie, "I wiss you'd ask Him to send that dream back again to-night—to presh on my byains an' *make* it come back, and then let me stay asleep until I yetted up all the candy I gotted into my pockets an' hands."

The appearance of the chambermaid, who came to dress the boys for breakfast, put an end to the conversation; but Mrs. Burton determined that it should be renewed at the earliest opportunity, or, rather, that her discoveries of her own shortcomings as a teacher of children should lead to an early and practical reformation.

The fit of mental abstraction into which this resolution

threw her was the cause of a silence which puzzled her husband considerably, for he could plainly see by her face that no ordinary affair was at the bottom of her reticence, and that what in men would be called temper was equally absent from her heart. In fact, the result upon Mrs. Burton's face and actions was so beneficial that the lady's husband determined to plead toothache as an excuse to remain at home for a day and look at her.

The mere suggestion, however, elicited from Mrs. Burton the mention of so many absolute necessities which could be procured only in the city and by her husband, that the young man departed by a train even earlier than the one upon which he usually traveled, and with sensations very like those of a person who has been forcibly ejected from his residence.

Then Mrs. Burton led her nephews into the sitting-room, seated herself, placed an arm tightly about each little boy, and said :

"Children, is there anything that you would very much like to know?"

"Yesh," answered Toddie, promptly. "*I'd* like to know what we're goin' to have for dinner to-day!"

"And I," said Budge, "would like to know when we're all goin' for a ride again."

"I don't mean silly things of that sort," said Mrs. Burton, "but——"

"*Ain't* silly fings," said Toddie. "Theysh what makesh ush happy."

Mrs. Burton made a mental note of the justice of the rebuke, and of its connection with the subject of which her heart was already full; but she was still Alice Mayton Burton, a lady whose perceptions could not easily prevent her from following the paths which she had already laid out for herself, so she replied :

"I know they are; but I want to teach you whatever you want to learn about matters of more importance."

"Do you mean that you want to play school?" asked Budge. "Papa don't think school is healthy for children in warm weather, an' neither do we."

"No, I don't want to play school, but I want to explain to you some of the things which you say you don't understand, though people tell you all about them. It makes Aunt Alice very unhappy to think that her dear little nephews are troubled about understanding things when they want so much to do so. Aunt Alice was once a little bit of a girl, and had just the same sort of trouble, and she remembers how uncomfortable it made her feel."

"My!" said Budge, changing his position until he could look into his aunt's eyes. "Did you ever have to wonder how big moons got to be little again, an' then have big folks tell you they chopped up the old moons an made stars of them, when you *knew* the story must be an awful whopper?"

"Yes," said Mrs. Burton.

"An' didn't you ever wunner what dinner was goin' to be made of, an' then have big folks just say 'never mind'?" asked Toddie.

"Yes," said Mrs. Burton, giving Toddie a light squeeze, "I've been through that, too."

"*My!*" said Budge, "you *was* awful little once, wasn't you? Well, did you ever have to wonder where God stood when He made the world out of nothin'?"

"An' did you ever have to fink how the sweet outsides got made onto date-stones an' peach-pits?" asked Toddie.

"Oh, yes," said Mrs. Burton.

"Then tell us all about 'em," said Budge.

"You asked me about dreams this morning, dear," said Mrs. Burton, addressing Budge, "and——"

"I know I did," said Budge; "but I'd rather know about dates an' peaches now. I can't dream any more till I go to bed; but I can buy dates inside of a quarter of an hour if you'll give me pennies. Oh, say—I'll tell you what—you send me to buy some, and then you can explain about 'em easier. It's so much nicer to *see* how things are than to have to think about them."

"I can't spare you now, dear, to go after dates; I may not have time to talk to you when you get back."

"Oh, we'd manage not to bother you," said Budge. "I think we could find out all about 'em ourselves—if we had enough of 'em to do it with, that is."

"Very well," said Mrs. Burton, compromising reluctantly; "I'll tell you about something else at present; then I will give you some money to purchase dates, and you may study them for yourselves."

"All right," said Budge. "Then tell us what makes your dog Terry always run away whenever we want him?"

"Because you tease him so badly whenever you catch him that you have made him hate you," said Mrs. Burton, delighted at the double opportunity to speak distinctly and impart a lesson in humanity.

"Now you's gettin' ready to say 'Don't,'" remarked Toddie, complainingly. "Can't little boysh lyne noffin' that hazn't got any mean old 'Don't' in it?"

"I guess so, poor little fellow," said Mrs. Burton, repenting at once of her success. "What would you like to know?"

Toddie opened his mouth and eyes, hung his head to one side, meditated for two or three minutes, and at last said:

"I—I—I—I—I wantsh to know whatsh the reason that when a little boy hazh been eatin' lotsh of buttananoes he can't eat any more, when he's been findin' out all the whole time how awful good they are?"

"Because his little stomach is full, and when one's stomach is full it knows enough to stop wanting anything."

"Then tummuks is gooses," said Toddie: "I wiss *I* was my tummuk dzust once; I'd show it how never to get tired of buttananoes."

"What *I* want to know," said Budge, "is how we have dreams, 'cause I don't know any more about it than I did before, after what you told me this morning."

"It's a hard thing to explain, dear," said Mrs. Burton, as she endeavored to frame a simple explanation. "We think with our brain, and when we sleep our brain sleeps too, though sometimes it isn't as sleepy as the rest of our body; and when it *is* a little wakeful it thinks the least bit, but it can't think straight, so each thought gets mixed up with part of some other thought."

"That's the reason I dreamed last night that a cow was sittin' in your rocking-chair readin' an atlas, then," said Budge; "but what made me think about cows an' rockin'-chairs an' atlases at all?"

"That's one of the things which we can't explain about dreams." said Mrs. Burton. "We seem to remember something that we have seen at some other time, and our memories jumble against each other when two or three come at a time."

"Then some night when I'ze asleep, I'm goin' to fink about buttananoes, an' red-herrings, an' ice-cream, an' sour-grass, an' hard-boiled eggs, an' candy, an' fried hominy, an' *won't* I hazh a lovaly little tea-party in bed, if all my finks djumbles togevver? An' I won't djcam about any uvver little boy wif me at all."

"When I dreams about dear little dead brother Phillie then," said Budge, "don't I do anything but just remember him?—don't he come down from heaven and see me in my bed?"

"I imagine not, dear," said Mrs. Burton.

"Then what makes him look so white and sunny, an' smile so sweet, an' flap his dear little white wings close to my face, so I can touch 'em?" asked Budge.

"I suppose it is because—because you have thought of him looking that way," said Mrs. Burton, drawing Budge closer to her side, to hide the wistfulness of his face from her own eyes. "You've seen pictures of angels all in white, with graceful wings, and you've thought of little brother Phil looking that way."

"Oh, dear!" exclaimed Budge, burying his face in his aunt's robe and bursting into tears. "I wish I hadn't tried to find out about dreaming. I don't *ever* want to learn about anything else. If dear little angel Phillie is only a piece of a think in my brain when I'm asleep, then there isn't nothing that's any thing. I always *thought* it was funny that he began to go away as soon as I began to wake up."

"*Cows* don't go 'way when *I* wakes up from dreamin

about 'em," said Toddie; "I 'members 'em all day, an' sees 'em whenever I don't want to."

Mrs. Burton could not repress a smile, while Budge raised his head, and said:

"Well, I suppose it's no good to be unhappy; we'd better have fun than think about things that's awful sad. Can't you think of some new kind of a play for us?"

"I'm afraid I can't think of any at this moment," said Mrs. Burton.

"Suppose you play store," said Budge, "an' keep lots of nice things, like cakes an' candies, an' let us buy 'em of you for pins. Oh, yes! an' you give us the pins to buy 'em with."

"An' do it 'fore it getsh dinner-time, so the fings you sell us can get out of the way in time, so we can get empty in time to get fullded up at dinner."

"I can't do that," said Mrs. Burton, "because it would give you little boys an excuse to eat between meals."

"Then tell us stories—no, make a menagerie for us—oh, no! *I'll* tell you what—make believe it was *our* house, an' you were comin' to visit us, and we'll bring you up cake an' coffee to rest yourself with."

"I—I'm afraid I smell some little mice!" said Mrs. Burton.

"In the moush-trap?" inquired Toddie. "Oh! get em for ush to play wif!"

"*Tell* you what," said Budge; "you can tell us that funny story about the man that had dogs for doctors."

"Dogs for doctors?" echoed Mrs. Burton.

"Yes," said Budge; "don't you know? He's in the Bible book."

"He may be," said Mrs. Burton, rapidly passing in review such Biblical dogs as she could remember, "but I don't know where."

"Why, don't you know?" continued Budge; "he was that man that was so poor that he had to eat crumbs, an' papa don't think he had any syrup with them either, like *we* do, when the cook gives us the crumbs out of the bread-box."

"Do you? Is it possible you mean Lazarus?" exclaimed Mrs Burton.

"Yesh," said Toddie, "that was him. 'Twasn't the Lazharus that began to live again after he was buried, though. *He* didn't have no dogs."

"The poor man, you mean," said Mrs. Burton, "was very sick and very poor, so that he had to be fed with the scraps that a rich man named Dives left at his own table. But the Lord saw him and knew what troubles he was having, and determined that the poor man should be happy after he died, to make up for the great deal of trouble he had when he was alive. So when poor Lazarus died the Lord took him right into heaven."

"Nobody has to eat table-scraps *there*, do they?" said Budge. "But say, Aunt Alice, what do they do in heaven with things that's left at the table? Isn't it wicked to throw them away up there?"

"Should fink they'd cut a hole in the floor of hebben 'an grop the scraps down froe, for poor peopie," said Toddie. "When I gets to be an andzel, an' gets done my dinners, I'm goin' to get up on the wall an' froe the rest over down into the world Only I must be tareho (careful) not to grop off myseff an' tumble into the wylde (world) again."

"Well, what *I* want to know is," said Budge, "how do they get things to eat for the angels? Do they have grocery stores, an' butcher shops, an' milk wagons up there?"

"Gracious, no!" exclaimed Mrs. Burton, her fingers instinctively moving toward her ears. "The Lord provides food in some way that we don't understand. But this poor Lazarus, after he became an angel, looked out of heaven, and who did he see, way off in the bad place, but the rich man whose leavings he had used to eat, for the rich man had died too. And the rich man begged Abraham——"

"I fought his name was Lazharus?" said Toddie.

"The poor man was named Lazarus," said Mrs. Burton; "but when he reached heaven he found good old

Abraham there, and Abraham took care of him. And the rich man begged Abraham to send Lazarus just to dip his finger in water and rub it on the rich man's lips, for he was thirsty."

"Why didn't he get a drink for himself?" asked Budge. "Can't rich people wait on themselves even when they die?"

"There is no water in the bad place," said Mrs. Burton. "That was why he was so thirsty."

"Goodnesh!" said Toddie. "Then how does little boysh make mud-pies there?"

"I hope no little boys ever go there," said Mrs. Burton. "But Abraham said: 'Not so, my friend. You had your good things while you were alive; now you must get along without anything But poor Lazarus must be made happy for he had very bad times when *he* was alive!"

"Is *that* the way it is?" asked Budge. "Then I guess Abraham will have to do lots for *me* when I die, for I have a good many bad times nowadays. Then what did the bothered old rich man do about it?"

"He told Abraham that he had some brothers that were alive yet, and he wished that an angel might be sent to tell them to be good, so as never to have to come to that dreadful place. But Abraham told him it wouldn't be of any use to send an angel. They had good books and preachers that would tell them what to do."

"An' did he have to go on bein' thirsty forever?" asked Budge.

"I suppose so," said Mrs. Burton, with a shudder, and realizing why it was that the doctrine of eternal torment was not more industriously preached from the pulpit.

"G'won!" remarked Toddie.

"That is all there is of it," said Mrs. Burton.

"Why, you didn't tell us a fing about the doctor-dogs," complained Toddie.

"Oh, those are not nice to tell about," said Mrs. Burton.

"I fink theysh dzust the nicest fing about the story," said Toddie. "Whenever I getsh a sore finger, I goes an' sits down by the back-door an' calls Terry. But I don't fink Terry's a very good doctor, 'cauzh he don't come when I wants him. One of these days when I getsh lotsh of soresh, like Jimmy McNally when he had the smallpox, an' Terry will want to see me *awful*, I won't let him see me a bit. Tell us 'nother story."

The sound of harp and fiddle came to Mrs. Burton's rescue, and the boys hurried to the front of the house to behold a couple of very small, peripatetic Italians who were doing their utmost to teach adults the value of peace and quietness.

Budge and Toddie listened to the whole *répertoire* of the couple, *encored* every selection, bestowed in payment the pennies their aunt gave them for the purpose, and then proposed to follow the musicians on their route through the town ; but their aunt stopped them.

"What do those little fellows do with all the pennies they get ?" asked Budge. "Do they buy candy with them ?"

"My ! What lotsh of candy they must have !" exclaimed Toddie.

"I suppose they take their money home to their papas and mammas," said Mrs. Burton, "for they are very poor people. Perhaps the parents of those two poor little boys are sick at this very moment, and are looking anxiously for the return of their little boys who are so far away." (Mem. The first report of the Society for the Prevention of Cruelty to Children had not been published at that time.)

"An' do the little boys make all that music dzust 'cauzh they love somebody ?" asked Toddie.

"Yes, dear," said Mrs. Burton.

"But folks always gets paid by the Lord for doin' things for other folks, don't they, Aunt Alice ?" asked Budge.

"Yes, dear old fellow," said Mrs. Burton.

"One fing nysh about them little boysh," remarked Toddie, "ish that, when their papas an' mammas is sick, there isn't anybody to tell the little boysh not to get their shoes dusty. Dzust see how they walksh along in the middle of the street, kicking up the dust, an' nobody to say 'Don't!' to 'em, an' nobody skrong enough to spynk 'em for it when they gets home. I wisses I was a musicker."

"Well, they're gone now," sighed Budge, "and we want something else to make us happy. Say, Aunt Alice, why don't you have a horse an' carriage like mamma, so that you could take us out ridin'?"

"Uncle Harry isn't rich enough to keep good horses and carriages." said Mrs. Burton, "and he doesn't like poor ones."

"Why, how much does good horses cost?" asked Budge. "I think Mr. Blanner's horses are pretty good, but papa says they'd be dear at ten cents apiece."

"I suppose a good horse costs three or four hundred dollars," said Mrs. Burton.

"My—y—y!" exclaimed Budge. "That's more money than it cost our Sunday-school to pay for a missionary! Which is goodest—horses or missionaries?"

"Missionaries, of course," said Mrs. Burton, leaving the piazza, with a dim impression that she had, during the morning, answered a great many questions with very slight benefit to any one.

The boys cared for themselves until lunch-time, and then returned with rather less appetite than was peculiar to them. The new siege of questioning which their aunt had anticipated was postponed ; each boy's mind seemed to be in the reflective, rather than the receptive, attitude.

After lunch they hastily disappeared, without any attempt on the part of their aunt to prevent them, for Mrs. Burton had arranged to make, that afternoon, one of the most important of calls. Mrs. Congressman Weathervane had been visiting a friend at Hillcrest, and Mrs. Weathervane's mother and Mrs. Burton's grandmother had been school-day acquaintances, and Mrs. Mayton would have come from the city to pay her respects to the descendant of the old friend of the family, but some of the infirmities of age prevented. And Mrs. Mayton instructed her daughter to call upon Mrs. Weathervane as a representative of the family, and Mrs. Burton would rather have lost her right hand or her new spring hat than have disregarded such a command. So she had hired a carriage and devised an irreproachable toilet, and recalled and tabulated everything she had ever heard about the family of the lady who had become Mrs. Weathervane.

The carriage arrived, and no brace of boys dashed from unexpected lurking-places to claim a portion of its seats. The carriage rolled off in safety, and Mrs. Burton fell into an impromptu service of praise to the kind Power, which often blesses us when we least expect to be blessed. The carriage reached the house where Mrs. Weathervane was visiting, and the terrible Mrs. Weathervane turned out to be one of the most charming of young women, before whose sunny temperament Mrs. Burton's assumed dignity melted like the snow of May, and her store of venerable family anecdotes disappeared at once from the memory which had guarded them so carefully.

But joy is never unalloyed in this wicked world. While the couple were chatting merrily under the influence of that sense of "affinity," which loathsome men rant about and sweet women discover among themselves, and Mrs. Weathervane was insisting that Mrs. Burton should visit her at Washington during the session, and Mrs. Burton was trying to persuade Mrs. Weathervane to accept the Burton hospitality for at least a day or two, there arose under the window the squeak of the violin and the wail of some badly-played wind instrument.

"Those wretched little Italians!" exclaimed Mrs. Weathervane. "For which of our sins, I wonder, are we condemned to listen to them?"

"If they come as punishment for sins," said Mrs. Burton, "how wicked I must be, for this is my second experience with them to-day. They were at my house for half an hour this morning."

"And you are sweet of disposition this afternoon?" said Mrs. Weathervane. "Oh! I *must* spend a day or two with you, and take some lessons in saintly patience."

Mrs. Burton inclined her head in acknowledgment, and Mrs. Weathervane approached some other topic, when the violin under the window gave vent to a series of terrible groans, while the wind instrument, apparently a flute, shrieked discordantly in three notes an octave apart.

"An attempt to execute something upon one string, I suppose," said Mrs. Weathervane, "and the execution is successful only as criminal executions are. What should be done to the little wretches? And yet one can't help giving them money; did you see the story of their terrible life in the papers this week? It seems they are hired in Italy by dreadful men, who bring them here, torture them into learning their wretched tunes, and then send them out to play and beg. They are terribly whipped if they do not bring home just so much money every day."

"The poor little things!" exclaimed Mrs. Burton. "I hadn't heard of that before. I'm glad to remember that I gave them a good many pennies this morning. I must have had an intuition of their fate, for I'm certain I had no musical enjoyment to be paid for. These little children can hardly be as old as some in nurseries, either."

"No, indeed," said Mrs. Weathervane, going to the window. "The elder of these two boys cannot be more than six, while the younger may be four; and the older looks *so* sad, so introspective. The younger—poor little fellow—has only expectancy in *his* countenance. He is looking up to all the windows for the pennies that he expects to be thrown to him. He has probably not had so hard an experience as his companion, for his instrument is only a common whistle. Think of the frauds which their masters practice upon the tender-hearted! The idea of sending out a child with a common whistle, on the pretense of making music!"

"It's perfectly dreadful!" said Mrs. Burton.

"Then to think what the parents of some of these children may have been," continued Mrs. Weathervane. 'The older of this couple has really many noble lines in his face, did not the long-drawn agony of separation and abuse inscribe deeper ones there. The smaller one, vilely dirty as he is, has a very picturesque head and figure. He is smiling now. Oh! what *wouldn't* I give if some artist could catch his expression for me!"

"Really," exclaimed Mrs. Burton, approaching the window, "I hadn't noticed so many charms about them; but I shall be glad to have them pointed out to me. Mercy!"

"What *can* be the matter?" murmured Mrs. Weathervane, as her visitor fell back from the window and dropped into a chair.

"They're — my — nephews!" gasped Mrs. Burton. "Oh, what *shall* I do with those dreadful children?"

"Stolen from home?" inquired Mrs. Weathervane, apparently discerning a marvelous romance within reaching distance.

"No—oh, no!" said Mrs. Burton. "I left them at home an hour or two ago. I can't imagine why they should have taken this freak, unless because boys will be dreadful, no matter what is done for them. I suppose," she continued, hurrying to the window, "that Budge has his uncle's violin, which I think is fully as dear to its owner as his wife is. Yes, he has it! Boys!" exclaimed Mrs. Burton, appearing at the piazza-door, "go directly home."

At the sound of their aunt's voice the boys looked up with glad smiles of recognition, while Budge exclaimed: "Oh, Aunt Alice! we've played at lots of houses, an' we've got nearly a dollar. We told everybody we was playin' to help Uncle Harry buy a horse an' carriage!"

"Go home!" repeated Mrs. Burton "Go by the back road, too. *I* am going myself right away—be sure that I find you there when I return"

Slowly and sadly the amateurs submitted to the fateful decree, and moved toward home, while Mrs. Weathervane bestowed a sympathetic kiss upon her troubled visitor. A great many people came to doors and windows to see the couple pass by, but what was public interest to a couple whose motive had been rudely destroyed? So dejected was their mien as they approached the Burton mansion, and so listless was their step that the dog Terry who had mounted guard at the front door, gave only an inquiring wag of his tail, and did not change his position as the boys passed over the door-mat upon which he lay. A moment or two later a carriage dashed up to the door, and Mrs. Burton descended, hurried into the house, and exclaimed:

"How dared you to do such a vulgar, disgraceful thing?"

"Well," said Budge, "that's another of the things we don't understand much about, even after we're told. We thought we could be just as good to you an' Uncle Harry as dirty little Italian boys are to their papas an' mammas, an' when we tried it, you made us go straight home."

"Dzust the same fing as sayin' 'Don't' at us," remarked Toddie.

"An' after we got a whole lot of money, too!" said Budge. "Papa says some big men don't get more than a dollar in a day, an' *we* got most a dollar in a little bit of a while. It's *partly* because we was honest though, I guess, an' told the troof everywhere—we told everybody that we wanted the money to help Uncle Harry to buy a horse an' carriage."

Uncle Harry himself, moved by his aching tooth, had returned from New York in time to hear, unperceived, the last portion of Budge's explanation, after which he heard the remainder of the story from his wife. His expression as he listened, his glance at his nephews, and his frantic examination of his beloved violin, gave the boys to understand how utter is sometimes the failure of good intentions to make happy those persons for whose benefit they are exerted. The sombre reflections of the young men were unchanged by anything which occurred during the remainder of the afternoon, and when they retired, it was with a full but sorrowful heart that Budge prayed: "Dear Lord, I've been scolded again for tryin' to do somethin' real nice for other people. I guess it makes me know something about how the good prophets an' Jesus felt. Please don't let *me* have to be crucified for doin' good, for Christ's sake, Amen."

And Toddie prayed: "Dee Lord, there's some more 'Dont' been said to me, an' I fink Aunt Alice ought to be 'shamed of herself. Won't you please make her so? Amen."

CHAPTER VII.

" THAT," murmured Mrs. Burton as she completed her toilet on Tuesday morning, and prepared to descend to the breakfast-table, "promises a pleasant day." Then, in a louder tone, she said to her husband: "Harry, just listen to those dear children singing! Aren't their voices sweet?"

"'Sing before breakfast, cry before dark,'" grunted Mr. Burton, quoting a popular saying.

"For shame!" exclaimed Mrs. Burton. "And when they're singing sweet little child-hymns, too. There! they're starting another."

Mrs. Burton took the graceful, listening attitude peculiar to ladies, and her husband stood stock-still in the military, yet idiotic, position of "attention," and both heard the following *morceau*:

"I want—to be—an an—gel
An' with—the an—gels stand;
A crown—upon—my fore—head
A hop—per in—my hand."

"Hopper—h'm—like enough," said Mr. Burton. "They

refer to the hind-leg of a grasshopper, my dear. The angelic life would be indeed dreary to those youngsters without some such original plaything."

"You ought to be ashamed of yourself," said the lady. "I hope you won't suggest any such notion to them. I don't believe they would ever have had so many peculiar views about the next world if some one hadn't exerted an improper influence—you and your brother-in-law, Tom Lawrence, their father, for instance."

"Well," said Mr. Burton, devoting himself to his hair-brush, "if they are so susceptible to the influences of others, I suppose *you* have them about reformed in most respects? You have had entire charge of them for seven days now."

"Six—only six," corrected Mrs. Burton, hastily. "I wish——"

"That there really *was* one day less for them to remain?" said Mr. Burton, looking his wife full in the face.

Mrs. Burton dropped her eyes quickly, trying first to turn in search of something she did not want, but her husband knew his wife's nature too much to be misled by this ruse. Putting as much tenderness in his voice as he knew how to do, he said:

"Little girl, tell the truth now; haven't *you* learned more than they have?"

Mrs. Burton still kept her eyes out of range of those of her husband, but replied, with admirable composure:

"I have learned a great deal, as one must always do when brought in contact with a new subject, but the acquired knowledge of an adult is the source of new power, and of more knowledge to be imparted."

Mr. Burton contemplated his wife with curiosity which soon made place for undisguised admiration, but when he turned his face again to the mirror he could see in its expression nothing but pity. Meanwhile the cessation of the children's songs, the confused patter of little feet upon the stair, and an agonized yelp from the dog Terry, indicated that the boys had left their chamber. Then the Burtons heard their own door-knob turned, an indignant kick which followed the discovery that the door was bolted, and then a shout of—

"Say!"

"What's wanted?" asked Mr. Burton.

"I wanted to come in," answered Budge.

"Me, too," piped Toddie.

"What for?" demanded Mr. Burton.

A moment of silence ensued, and then Budge answered:

"Why, because we *do*. I should think *any*body would understand that without asking."

"Well, we bolted the door because we didn't want any

one to come in," answered Mrs. Burton. "I should think anybody could understand *that* without asking."

"Oh!" replied Budge. "Well, I'll tell you what we want to come in for; we want to tell you something perfectly lovely."

"Do you wish to listen to an original romance, my dear?" asked Mr. Burton.

"Certainly," replied the lady.

"And break your resolution to teach them that our chamber is not a general ante-breakfast gathering-place."

"Oh, they won't infer anything of the kind if we admit them just once," said Mrs. Burton.

"H'm—we won't count this time," quoted Mr. Burton from "Rip Van Winkle," with a most suggestive smile, which was instantly banished by a frown from his wife. Mr. Burton dutifully drew the bolt, and both boys tumbled into the room.

"We were both leaning against the door," explained Budge; "that's why we dropped over each other; we knew you'd let us in."

Mr. Burton gave his wife another peculiar look, which the lady affected not to notice, as she asked:

"What is the lovely thing you were going to tell us?"

"Why——"

"I—I—I—I—I——" interrupted Toddie.

"Tod, be still," commanded Budge. "I began it first."

"But I *finked* it fyst," expostulated Toddie.

"I'll tell you what, then, Tod—I'll tell 'em about it an' you worry 'em to do it—*that's* fair, isn't it?" and then, without awaiting the result of Toddie's deliberations Budge continued:

"What *we* want is to have a picnic Papa'll lend you the carriage, and we'll get in it and go up to the Falls, and have a lovely day of it. That's just the nicest place I ever saw. You can swing us in the big swing there, an' take us in swimming, and row us in a boat, and buy us lemonade at the hotel, and we can throw stones in the water, an' paddle, an' catch fish an' run races All these other things—not the first ones I told you about—we can do for ourselves, an' you an' Aunt Alice can lie on the grass under the trees an' smoke cigars an' be happy, 'cause you've made *us* happy. That's the way papa does. An' you must take lots of lunch along, 'cause little boys gets pretty empty feeling when they go to such places. Oh, yes—an' you can throw Terry in the water an' make him swim after sticks—I'll bet he can't get away *there* without our catching him."

"But the lunch has got to be lots," said Toddie, "else there won't be any fun—not one bittie. An' you'll take us, won't you? We'ze been dreadful good all morning I'ze singed Sunday songs until my froat's all sandy."

"All what?" asked Mrs. Burton.

"Sandy," replied Toddie. "Don't you know how funny it feels to rub sand between your hands when you hazhn't got djuvs (gloves) on? If you don't I'll go bring you in some."

"I guess your aunt will take your word for it." said Mr. Burton, as his wife did not respond

"An' we'll be awful tired after the picnic's done," said Budge, "an' you can hold us in your arms in the carriage all the way back. That's the way papa an' mamma does."

"Thank you," said Mr. Burton. "That *will* be an inducement. And it explains why your papa can make a new suit look old quicker than any other man of my acquaintance."

"And why your mother always has a polonaise or overskirt to clean or mend," said Mrs. Burton.

"It's all told now, Tod," said Budge. "Why don't you worry 'em."

Toddie clasped his aunt's skirts affectionately, and said, in most appealing tones:

"You'se a-goin' to, izhn't you?"

"Papa says it was always easier for you to say 'yes than 'no,'" remarked Budge, addressing his uncle, "an'——"

A fine reputation your brother-in-law gives you," remarked Mrs. Burton.

"An' I once heard a lady say she thought *you* said yes' pretty easy," continued Budge, addressing his aunt. "I thought she meant something that you said to Uncle Harry by the way she talked." Mrs. Burton flushed angrily, but Budge continued: "An' you ought to be as good to us as you are to him, 'cause he's a big man, an' don't have to be helped every time he wants any fun. Besides, you've got him all the time, but you can only have us four days longer—three days besides to-day."

"Another paraphrase of Scripture—application perfect," remarked Mr. Burton to his wife. "Shall we go?"

"Can *you* go?" asked the lady, suddenly grown radiant.

"I suppose—I *know* I can!" replied Mr. Burton, fondly, assuming that the anticipation of a day in his society was the sole cause of his wife's joy.

Mrs. Burton knew his thoughts, but failed to correct them, guilty though she felt at her neglect. The idea that she would be practically relieved of responsibility during the day was the cause of her happiness. The children had always preferred the companionship of their uncle to that of his wife; she had at times been secretly mortified and offended at this preference: but during the week just ending she had entirely lost this feeling.

The announcement that their host and hostess thought favorably of the proposition was received by the boys with the most lively manifestations of delight, and for two hours no other two persons in the State were more busy than Budge and Toddie. Even their appetites gave way under the excitement, and their stay at the breakfast-table was of the shortest duration.

Budge visited his father and arranged for the use of the carriage, while Toddie superintended the packing of the lunch until the cook banished him from the kitchen, and protected herself from subsequent invasion by locking the door. Then both boys suggested enough extra baggage to fill a wagon, and volunteered instructions at a rate which was not retarded by the neglect with which their commands were received.

At length, however, the last package was taken into the carriage, and dog Terry was helped to a seat, and the party started. They had been *en route* about five minutes, when Budge remarked:

"Uncle Harry, I want a drink."

"Uncle Harry," said Toddie, "*I'm* 'most starved to deff—I didn't have hardly any breksup."

"Why not?" asked Mrs. Burton. "Wasn't there plenty on the table?"

"I doe know," said Toddie, looking inquiringly into his aunt's face as if to refresh his memory.

"Weren't you hungry at breakfast-time?" continued Mrs. Burton.

"I—I—I—I—why, yesh—I mean my tummuk wazh hungry but my toofs wasn't—thatsh the way it wazh. An' I guesh what I'd better have now is sardines an' pie."

"Ethereal creature!" exclaimed Mrs. Burton, giving Toddie a cracker or two.

"I didn't remember that *I* was hungry," remarked Budge, "but Tod's talking about it reminds me. An' I'd like that drink, too."

Budge also received some crackers, and the carriage was stopped near a convenient well. The descent of Mr. Burton from the carriage compelled the dog Terry to change his base, which operation was so impeded by skillful efforts on the part of the boys that Terry suddenly leaped to the ground and started for home, followed by a remonstrance from Toddie, while Budge remarked:

"*He* won't ever go to heaven, Terry won't—he don't like to make people happy."

Away went the carriage again, and it had reached the extreme outskirts of the town when Toddie said:

"I'm *awful* fursty."

"Why did't you drink when Budge did?" demanded Mr. Burton.

"'Cauzh I didn't want to," replied Toddie. "I izhn't like old choo-choos (locomotives) that gets filled up dzust because they comes to a watering-playsh. I only likesh to drink when I'zhe fursty; an' I'zhe fursty now."

Another well was approached, and Toddie drank about two swallows of water, replying to his aunt's declaration that he couldn't have been thirsty at all by the explanation:

"I doezn't hold very much. I izhn't like horsesh, that can dzink whole pailsful of water, an' then hazh room for gwash (grass). But I guesh I'zhe got room for some cake."

"Then I'll give you another cracker," said Mr. Burton.

"Don't want one," said Toddie. "Cwacker couldn't push itself down as easy as cake."

"I *do* believe," said Mrs. Burton, "that the child's animal nature has taken complete possession of him. Eating and mischief has been the whole of his life during the week, and he used to be so sweetly fanciful and sensitive."

"Children's wits are like the wind, my dear," said Mr. Burton. "'Thou canst not tell whence it cometh nor whither it goeth;' you set your sails for it, and behold it isn't there, but when you're not expecting it down comes the gale."

"A gale!" echoed Budge. "That's what we're goin' to have to-day."

"Izn't neiver," said Toddie. "Goin' to hazh a pic-nic."

"Well, gales and picnics is the same thing," said Budge.

"No, they izhn't," said Toddie. "Gales is kind o' rough,

but picnics is nice. Galesh is like rough little boysh—like *you*—but picnics is nice, like dear little sister-babies."

"Oh, dear," sighed Budge, "we haven't seen that baby for two days—let's go right back an' look at her."

"Budge, Budge," remonstrated Mrs. Burton; "try to be content with what you have, and don't always be longing for something else. You can go to see her when we return."

"*I* can see her *wivout* going back," said Toddie. "I can see anybody I wantsh to, dzust whenever I pleash."

"Don't be silly, Toddie," remonstrated Mrs. Burton, in spite of a warning nudge from her husband.

"How do you see them, Toddie?" asked Mr. Burton.

"Why, I dzust finks a fink about 'em, an' then they comezh wight inshide of my eyezh, an' I sees 'em. I see lotsh of peoples that-a-way. I sees AbrahammynIsaac, an' Bliaff, an' little Dave, an' the Hebrew children, an' George Washitton hatchetin' down his papa's tree, whenever I finks about 'em. Oh, there goez a wabbit! Letsh stop an' catch him."

"Oh, no, let him go," said Mr. Burton. "Perhaps he's going home to dinner, and his family are all waiting at the table for him."

"My!" said Toddie, opening his eyes very wide, and keeping silence for at least two minutes. Then he said, "*I* saw a wabbit family eatin' dinner once. They had a little bittie of a table, an' little bits of chairzh, and the papa wabbit ashkted a blessin', an'——"

"Toddie, Toddie, don't tell fibs!" said Mrs. Burton.

"Izn't tellin' fibs," said Toddie. "An' a little boy wabbit said, 'Papa, I wantsh a dzink.' So his father took a little tumbler, dzust about as big as a fimble, an' held a big leaf up sideways so the dew would run off into the tumbler, an' he gived it to the little boy wabbit. An' when they got done dinner, the mamma wabbit gave each of the little boy wabbits a strawberry to suck An' none of 'em had to be told to put on the napkins, 'cause they only had one dress, and that was a color that didn't show dyte, like mamma says *I* ought to have."

"Were all the little rabbits boys—no girls at all?" asked Mr Burton.

"Yesh, there was a little sister baby; but she wazh too little to come to the table, so the mamma-wabbit held her in her lap and played 'Little Pig Went to Market' on her little bits of toes. Then the sister-baby got tired, an' the mamma-wabbit wocked it in a wockin'-tsair, an' sung to it 'bout—

> 'Papa gone a-huntin',
> To get a little wabbit-skin
> To wap the baby buntin'—baby wabbit—in.'

Then the baby-wabbit got tied of its mamma, an' got down and cwept around on itsh handsh an' kneesh, an' didn't dyty its djess at all or make its knees sore a bit, 'cauzh there wazh only nice leaves an' pitty fynes (ferns) for it to cweep on, instead of ugly old carpets. Say, do you know *I* was a wabbit once?"

"Why, no," said Mr. Burton. "Do tell us about it."

"Harry!" remonstrated Mrs. Burton.

"*He* believes it, my dear," explained her husband. "He has his 'sweetly fanciful' mood on now, that you were moaning for a few moments ago. Go on, Toddie."

"Why, I was a wabbit, and lived all by myself in a hole froo the bottom of a tree. An' sometimes uvver wabbits came to see me, an' we all sat down on our foots an' bowed our ears to each uvver. Dogsh came to see me sometimes, but I dzust let them wing the bell an' didn't ask 'em to come in. An' then a dzentleman came an' asked me to help him make little boysh laugh in a circus. So I runned around the ring, and picked up men an' fings with my tchunk——"

"Why, rabbits don't have trunks, Toddie," observed Mr. Burton.

"I know it," said Toddie, "but I turned into a ephalant (elephant). An' I got lotsh of hay an' fings wif my tchunk, an' folks gave me lotsh of cakes an' candies to see me eat 'em wif my tchunk, an' I was so big I could hold 'em all, an' I didn't have any mamma ephalant to say 'Too muts cake an' candy will make you sick, Toddie.'"

"Anything more?" asked Mr. Burton. "We can stand nearly anything."

"Well," said Toddie reflectively, "I gotted to be a lion then, and had to roar so much that my froat gotted all sandy, so I got turned into a little boy again, an' I was awful hungry. I guess 'twas djust now."

"Can you resist *that* hint, my dear?" said Mr. Burton.

Mrs Burton, with a sigh, opened a basket and gave Toddie a piece of cake, and the young man remarked:

"Thish izh to pay me for tellin' the troof about all them fings, izhn't it?"

About this time the party reached Little Falls, and Budge remarked:

"I suppose lunch 'll be the first thing?"

"No," said Mrs. Burton; "we won't have lunch until our usual lunch-hour."

But you can have all the drinks you want," said Mr. Burton. "There's a whole river full of water."

"Oh, I don't feel as if I'd ever be thirsty again," said Budge. "But I wish Terry was here to swim in after sticks. *You* do it, won't you?—you play dog an' I'll play Uncle Harry an' throw things to you."

By this time Toddie had sought the waters' edge, and, taking a stooping position, was looking for fish. The shelving stone upon which he stood was somewhat moist, and Toddie was so intent on his search that he stooped forward considerably, and suddenly there was heard a splash and a howl, and Toddie was seen in the river in water knee-deep. To rescue him was the work only of a moment, but to stop his tears was no such easy matter.

"What *is* to be done?" exclaimed Mrs. Burton.

"Take off his shoes and stockings and let him run bare-footed," said Mr. Burton. "The day is warm, and he can't catch cold."

"Why!" exclaimed Toddie, "Izh I goin' to be bare-foot all day? I wishes thish river wazh right by our housh—I'd tumble in every day. Budgie, Budgie, if you wantsh fun djust go tumble splash into the river."

But Budge had strolled away, and was tugging at some moss in a crevice of rock. Here his aunt found him, and he explained, toiling as he talked:

"I thought—this—would make such—a—lovely cushion for—for you to sit on."

The last word and the final tug were concurrent, and the moss gave way; so did Budge, and with a terrific scream, for a little snake had made his home under the moss, and was expressing considerable indignation, in his own way, at being disturbed.

"I won't never do nothing for nobody again," screamed Budge. "I'll see that snake every time I shut my eyes, now."

"You poor dear little fellow," said Mrs Burton, caressing him tenderly. "I wish Aunt Alice could do something to make you forget it."

"Well, you *can't*," sobbed Budge, "unless—unless, maybe, a piece of pie would do it. It wouldn't do any harm to try, I s'pose?"

Mrs Burton hurried to unpack a pie, as her husband remarked that Budge was born to be a diplomatist. Looking suspiciously about, for fear that Toddie might espy Budge's prescription, and devise some ailment which it would exactly suit, she discovered that Toddie was out of sight.

"Oh, he's gone, Harry! Hurry and find him. Perhaps he's gone above the Falls. I do wish we had gone further down the river!"

Mr. Burton took a lively double-quick up and along the bank of the river, but could see nothing of his nephew.

At length, however, above the roar of the falling water, he heard a shrill voice singing over again a single line of an old Methodist hymn,

"Roar—ing riv—ers, migh—ty foun—tains!"

Following the sound, he peeped over the bank, and saw Toddie in a sunny nook of rocks just below the Falls, and i the very ecstasy of delight. He would hold out his hands as if to take the fall itself; then he would throw back his head and render his line with more force; then he would dance frantically about, as if his little body was unable to comfortably contain the great soul within it.

Suddenly coming up the sands below the cliff appeared Mrs. Burton, whose apprehensions had compelled her to join in the search.

"Oh, Aunt Alish!" exclaimed Toddie, discovering his aunt, and hurrying to grasp her hand in both of his own; "dzust see the water dance! Do you see all the lovely lights that the Lord's lit in it? Don't you wiss you could get in it, an' fly froo it, an' have it shake itself all over you, an' shake yourself in it, an' shake it all off of you, an' then fly into it aden? Theresh placesh like this up in hebben. I *know*, 'cauzh I *saw* 'em—one time I did. An' all the andzels staid around 'em, an' flew in an' out, an' froo, an' laughed like everyfing. An' Jesus sat right up on the bank lookin' at 'em, an' laughed wif 'em!"

Mr. Burton concealed all of himself but his eyes and hat as he observed the impending conflict of ideas; but no conflict ensued, for Mrs. Burton snatched her nephew and kissed him soundly. But Toddie wriggled away, exclaiming:

"Don't do that, or I'll get some uvver eyes when I don't want 'em!"

How long Toddie's ecstasy might have endured the Burtons never knew, for a tremendous clatter of horse-hoofs on the road attracted Mr. Burton, and, looking hastily back, he beheld one of his brother's horses galloping wildly back toward Hillcrest, while, just letting go of a rein-strap, the form of the boy Budge, enlivened the dust of the roadway, while his voice rose shrilly above the thunder of the falling waters.

With an old cavalryman's natural instinct, Mr. Burton attempted first to catch the horse; but the animal shied so successfully, and had such a clear stretch of roadway before him, that humanity soon had Mr. Burton's heart for its own, and he hurried to the assistance of Budge.

"I—boo-hoo—was just goin' to lead the—boo-hoo-hoo—horse down to water like—boo-hoo-hoo-hoo—ah—like papa does, when he—*oh!* how my elbow hurts!—just pulled away an' went off. An' I caught the strap to stop him, an'—oh! *ow*—he just pulled me along on my mouth in the dirt about ten miles, I reckon. I swallowed all the dirt I could, but I guess I've got a mouthful left."

Mr. Burton hurriedly unharnessed the other horse, and started, riding bareback, in search of the runaway, while his wife, who had intuitively known of some trouble in the air, hurried up the cliff with Toddie, and led both boys to the shadow of the carriage, with instructions to be perfectly quiet until their uncle returned.

"Can't we talk?" asked Toddie.

"No; not unless you need to for some particular purpose," said Mrs. Burton, who, like most other people in trouble, fought most earnestly against any form of diversion which should keep her from the extremity of worry. "Can't little boys' mouths *ever* be quiet?"

"Why, yes," said Budge, "when there's something in 'em to *keep* 'em still."

In utter desperation Mrs. Burton unpacked all the lunch-baskets and told the children to help themselves. As for her, she sought the roadside and gazed earnestly for her husband. Weary at last by hope deferred, she returned to the carriage to find that the boys had eaten all the pie and cake, drank the milk and ate the sugar which were to have formed part of some delicious coffee which Mr. Burton was to have made *à la militaire*, and had battered into shapelessness a box of sardines which they had attempted to open with a stone.

"You bad boys!" exclaimed Mrs. Burton. "Now what will your poor uncle have to eat when he comes back all tired, hungry and thirsty, and all because of your mischief, Budge."

"Why, we haven't touched the crackers, Aunt Alice," said Budge. "There's what he gave *us* when we said we was awful hungry, an' there's a whole river full of water to drink, like he told *us* about when he thought we was thirsty."

The information did not seem to console Mrs. Burton particularly, but she ventured to the roadside with the feeling that she could endure it to know that her husband was starving if she could only see him safe back again. The moments dragged wearily on, the boys grew restive and then cross, and finally, at about three in the afternoon, Mr. Burton reappeared. The runaway had nearly reached home, breaking a shoe *en route*, and his captor had found it necessary to seek a blacksmith. The horse he had rode had evidently never been broken to the saddle, and many had been the jeers of the village boys at his rider's apparent mismanagement. All that he knew now was that he was ravenously hungry.

"And the boys have eaten everything but the bread and crackers," gasped Mrs. Burton. "*I've* not eaten a mouthful."

"Goodness!" exclaimed Mr. Burton, feeling the boys' waistbelts; "did't they throw anything away?"

"Only down our froats," said Toddie.

"Then I'll go to the nearest hotel," said the disappointed man, "and get a nice dinner."

"We'll go too," said Budge. "Pie an' cake an' all such things don't fill people a bit on picnics."

"Then I guess a little emptiness will be the best for you," said Mr. Burton. "You remain here with your aunt."

"Well, hurry up, then," said Budge. "Here's the afternoon half gone, Aunt Alice says, and you haven't made us a whistle, or taken us in swimming, or let us catch fishes, or throwed big stones in the water for us, or anything."

Mr. Burton departed with becoming meekness, his nephew's admonition ringing in his ears, while the boys hovered solemnly about their aunt until she exclaimed:

"What *are* you acting so strangely for, boys?"

"Oh, we feel kind o' forlorn, an' want to be comforted," said Budge.

"Then will you comfort poor Uncle Harry when he comes back?" asked Mrs. Burton.

"Why, I heard him once tell you that *you* were his comfort," said Budge; "an' comforts oughtn't to be mixed up if folks is goin' to get all the good out of 'em—that's what papa says."

Mrs. Burton kissed both nephews, and asked them what she could do for them.

"I do' know," said Toddie.

Inspiration, pure and unadulterated, came to Mrs. Burton's assistance, and she answered:

"You may both do exactly as you please."

"Hooray!" shouted Budge.

"An you izhn't goin' to say 'Don't!' a single bit? asked Toddie.

"No," said Mrs. Burton.

"Why!" exclaimed both brothers, in unison.

Then they clasped hands, and walked slowly and

silently away. They even stopped to kiss each other, while Mrs. Burton looked on in silent amazement.

Was this really the result of not keeping a watchful eye—a badger eye, her husband termed it—upon children?

Then the boys still rambled quietly along, and finally sat down upon a large rock, put their arms around each other, and gazed silently at the scenery. They sat there until their uncle returned, and their aunt pointed out the couple to him. Then the adults insensibly followed the example set by the juveniles, and on the banks of the river sweet peace ruled for an hour, until old Sol, who once stood still to look at a fight, but never paused to contemplate humanity, conquered by the tender influences of nature, warned the party that it was time to return.

"It's time to go, boys," said Mr. Burton, with a sigh.

The words snapped the invisible thread that had held the children in exquisite captivity, and they were boys again in an instant, though not without a wistful glance at the Eden they were leaving.

"Now, Uncle Harry," said Budge, "there's always one thing that's got to be done before a picnic an' a ride is just right—an' *that* is, for me to drive the horses."

"An' me to hold the whip," said Toddie.

"Oh, I think you've done your whole duty to-day, both of you," said Mr. Burton, instinctively grasping the lines more tightly.

"But *we* don't," said Budge, "an' we know. Goin' *up* the mountain papa *always* lets us do it, an' he says the horses always know the minute *we* take 'em in hand."

"I shouldn't wonder," said Mr. Burton. "Well, here's a hill—take hold!"

Budge seized the reins, and Toddie took the whip from its socket. The noble animals at once sustained their master's statement, for they began to prance in a manner utterly unbecoming quiet family horses. Mrs. Burton clutched her hushand's arm, and Mr. Burton prudently laid his own hand upon the loop of the reins.

The crest of the hill was reached, Mr. Burton took the reins from the hand of his nephew, but Toddie made one final clutch at departing authority by giving the off horse a spirited cut. Tom Lawrence would never own a horse who needed even a touch of the whip, though that emblem of authority always adorned his carriage. When, therefore, this unfamiliar attention greeted them, the horse who was struck became gloriously indignant, and his companion sympathized with him, and the heels of both animals shot high in air, and then, at a pace which they themselves were powerless to arrest, the horses dashed down the rocky, rugged road. The top of a boulder, whose side had been cleanly washed, lay in the path of the carriage, and Mr. Burton gave the opposite rein a hasty twist about his hand as he tried to draw to the side of the road. But what was a boulder that equine indignation should regard it? The stone was directly in front and in line of the wheels. Mrs. Burton prepared for final dissolution by clasping her husband tightly with one arm, while with the other she clutched at the reins; the boys started the negro hymn "Oh, de rocky road to Zion," the wheels struck the boulder, four people described parabolic curves in air, and ceased only when their further progress was arrested by some bushes on the roadside, while the carriage righted itself, and was hurried home by the horses, while a party of pedestrians, two of whom were very merry, and two utterly reticent, completed their journey on foot, pausing only to bathe scratched faces at a brookside. And when, an hour later, two little boys had been in utter solitude preparing for bed, and their temporary guardians were alternately laughing and complaining over the incidents of the day, a voice was heard at the head of the stairs, saying:

"Uncle Harry, are we going to finish the picnic to-morrow? 'Cause we didn't get half through to-day. There's lots of picnicky things that we didn't get a chance to think about."

And another voice shouted:

"An' letsh take more lunch wif us. Izhe been awful hungry all day long."

CHAPTER VIII.

Only three more days," soliloquized Mrs. Burton, when the departure of her husband for New York and the disappearance of the boys gave her a quiet moment to herself. "Three more days, and then peace—and a lifelong sense of defeat! And by whom? By two mere infants in years, but in wisdom how mature! I erred in not taking them singly. When they are together, it's impossible to take their minds off their own childish affairs long enough to impress them with larger sense and better ways. But I *didn't* take them singly, and I *have* talked, and oh—stupidest of women!—I've blundered upon my husband for my principal listener. He gets along with them better than I do, and the exasperating thing about it is that he seems to do it without the slightest effort. How is it? They cling to him, mind him, sit by the roadside for an hour before train time just to catch the first glimpse of him, while I—am I growing uninteresting? Many women do after they marry, but I didn't think that I"—here Mrs. Burton extracted a tiny mirror from a vase on the mantle—"that I could be made stupid by marrying a loving old merry-heart like Harry!"

Mrs. Burton scrutinized her lineaments intently, first with suspicion, then with an indignant flush that brightened and strengthened them amazingly.

"Hell hath no fury like a woman scorned!"

once wrote a poet; but women—some women at least—have since then been discovering the nobler traits of their sex, so it came to pass that a wistful earnestness stole into Mrs. Burton's face as she studied it, and it softened every line, and, finally, breathed a slight mist over her eyes and parted her lips, in mute inquiry after that against which their owner had ceased to protest. Suddenly but softly little arm stole about her neck, and a little voice exclaimed, as she started with surprise:

"Aunt Alice, why don't you *always* look that way? There! now you're stoppin' it. Big folks is just like little boys, ain't they? Mamma says it's never safe to tell us we're good, 'cause we go an' stop it right away."

"When did you come in, Budge? How did you come so softly: Have you been listening? Don't you know it is very impolite to listen to people when they're not talking to you? Why, where are your shoes and stockings?"

"Why," said Budge, "I took 'em off so's—so's to get

some cake for a little tea-party without makin' a noise about it! You say our little boots make such an awful racket! But say, why don't you?"

"Why don't I what?" asked Mrs. Burton, her whole train of thought whisking out of sight at lightning speed.

"Why don't you always look like you did a minute ago? If you did, I wouldn't ever play or make trouble a bit. I'd just sit still all the time, and do nothin' but look at you."

"How did I look, Budge?" asked Mrs. Burton, taking the child into her arms.

"Why, you looked as if—as if—well, I don't 'zactly know. You looked like papa's picture of Jesus's mamma does, after you look at it a long time, an' nobody is there to bother you. I never saw anybody else look that way 'xcept my mamma, an' when she does it I don't ever say a word, else mebbe she'll stop."

"You can have the cake you came for," remarked Mrs. Burton.

"I don't want any cake," said Budge, with an impatient movement. "I don't want any tea-party. I want to stay with you, an' I want you to talk to me, 'cause you're beginnin' to look that way again." Here Budge nearly strangled his aunt in a tight embrace, and kissed her repeatedly.

"You darling little fellow," asked Mrs. Burton, returning the caresses, "do you know why I looked as I did? I was wondering why you and Toddie loved your Uncle Harry so much better than you did me, and why you always minded him and disobeyed me."

Budge was silent for a moment or two, then he sighed and answered:

"'Cause."

"Because of what?" asked Mrs. Burton. "You would make me very happy if you were to explain it to me."

"Well," said Budge, "'cause you're different."

"But Budge," argued Mrs. Burton, "I know a great many people who are not like each other, but I love them equally well."

"They ain't uncles an' aunts, are they?" asked Budge.

"No," replied Mrs. Burton; "but what has that to do with it?"

"And they're not folks you have to mind, are they?" continued Budge.

"N——no," said Mrs. Burton, descrying a dim light afar off, and looking intently there as if to see more of it.

"Do they want you to do things their way?" asked Budge.

"Some of them do," replied Mrs. Burton.

"An' do you do it?" continued the little questioner.

"Sometimes I do."

"You don't unless you want to, do you?"

"No," said Mrs. Burton, promptly.

"Well, neither do I," said Budge. "But when Uncle Harry wants me to do something, why somehow or other, I want to do it myself after awhile. I don't know why, but I do. An' I don't always when *you* tell me to. I love you ever so much when you ain't tellin' me things, but when you are, then they ain't ever what I want to do. That's all I know 'bout it. 'Xcept he don't want me to do such lots of thing as you do. He likes to see us enjoy ourselves; but sometimes I think you don't. We can't be happy only our way, an' our way seems to be like Uncle Harry's, an' yours ain't."

Mrs. Burton mused, and gradually her lips twitched back into their natural lines.

"There—you're stoppin' lookin' that way," said Budge, sighing and straightening himself. "I guess I *do* want the cake an' the tea-party."

"*Don't* go, Budgie dear," exclaimed Mrs. Burton, clasping the boy tightly. "When any one teaches you anything that you want very much to know, doesn't it make you happy?"

Oh, yes—lots," said Budge.

Well, then, if you try, perhaps you can teach Aunt Alice something that she wants very much to know"

"What!" exclaimed Budge. "A little boy teach a grown folks lady! My! I guess I'll stay."

"I want to understand all about this difference between your Uncle Harry and me," continued Mrs. Burton. "Do you think you minded him very well last summer?"

"That's too long ago for me to remember," said Budge. "But I didn't ever mind him unless I wanted to, or else had to, an' when I had to an' didn't want to, I didn't love him a bit. I just talked to papa about it when he got back home again, an' he said 'twas 'cause Uncle Harry didn't know us well enough, an' didn't always have time to find out all about us. Then *they* had a talk about it—papa and Uncle Harry did—in the library one day. I know they did, 'cause I was playin' blocks in a corner, an' I just stopped a-playin' an' listened to 'em. An' all at once papa said, 'Little pitchers!' an' said I'd oblige him very much if I'd go to the store an' buy him a box of matches. But I just listened a minute after I went out of the room, until I heard Uncle Harry say he'd been a donkey. I *knew* he was mistaken about that, so I went back an' told him he hadn't ever been any animals but what's in a menagerie, an' then they both laughed an' went out walkin', an' I don't know what they said after that. Only Uncle Harry's been awful good to me ever since, though sometimes I bother him when I don't mean to."

Mrs. Burton released one arm from her nephew and rested her head thoughtfully upon her hand. Budge looked up and exclaimed:

"There! You're looking that way again. Say, Aunt Alice, don't Uncle Harry love you *lots* of lots when you look so?"

Mrs. Burton recalled some evidence of such experiences, but before she could say so a small curly head came cautiously around the edge of the door, and then it was followed by the whole of Toddie, who exclaimed.

"I fink you's a real mean bruvver, Budgie. The tea-party's been all ready for you an' the cake, till I had to eat up all the strawberries to keep the nasty little ants from eatin' 'em. I yet up the cabbage-leaf plate they was in, too, to keep me from gettin' hungrier."

"There!" exclaimed Budge, springing from his aunt's lap; "that's just the way, whenever I'm lovin' to anybody, somethin' always goes and happens."

"Is that all you care for your aunt, then, Budge?" asked Mrs. Burton. "Is a tea-party worth more than me?"

Budge reflected for a moment. "Well," said he, "didn't *you* cry when *your* tea-party was spoiled last week on your burfday? To be sure your tea-party was bigger than ours, but then you're a good deal bigger than me, too, an' I haven't cried a bit."

Mrs. Burton saw the point, and was mentally unable to avoid it. For once that day, and likely enough the only time, an adult was placed in the position of a child, and had eyes with which to see that selfishness, physical or mental, had been at the bottom of most of her effoits for the children. The view was not a pleasant one, and grew more humiliating the longer it was presented. It was, perhaps, to banish it that she rose from her chair, brought from a closet in the dining-room a couple of pieces of the coveted cake, and gave one to each boy, saying:

"It isn't that Aunt Alice cares so much for her cake, dears, that she doesn't like you to have it between meals, but because it is bad for little boys to eat such heavy food excepting at their regular meals. There are grown people who were once happy little children, but now they are very cross all the while because their stomachs are all disordered by eating when they should not, and eating things which are richer and heavier than their bodies can use."

"Well," said Budge, crowding the contents of his mouth into his cheeks, "can we eat something plainer an' lighter to mix up with 'em inside of us? I should think charlotte-russe or whipped-cream would be about the thing; shall I ask the cook to fix some?"

"No," said Mrs. Burton, in haste. "Exercise would be better than anything else. I think you had better take a walk."

"Up to Hawkshnesht Rock?" suggested Toddie.

"Oh, yes!" exclaimed Budge. "An' you come with

us, Aunt Alice; perhaps you'll look that way again—*that* way, you know—an' I wouldn't like to lose any of it."

Mrs. Burton could not decline so delicate an invitation, and soon the trio were on the road, Mrs. Burton walking leisurely on the turf by the side, while the boys plowed their way through the dust of the middle of the road, pretending to be horses and succeeding so far as to create a dust-cloud which no team of horses could have excelled.

"Boys, boys!" shouted Mrs. Burton. "Is no one going to be company for me?"

"Oh—*I'll* be your gentleman," said Budge.

"I'll help," said Toddie, and both boys hurried to their aunt's side.

"Little boys," said Mrs. Burton, gently, "do you know that your mamma and papa have to pay a high price for the fun you have in kicking up dust? Look at your clothes; they must be sent to the cleaner's before they will ever again be fit to wear where respectable people can see you."

"Then," said Budge, "they're just right to give to poor little boys, and just think how glad they'll be. I guess they'll thank the Lord 'cause we ran in the dust."

"The poor little boys would have been just as glad to have had them while they were clean," said Mrs. Burton, "and the kindness would have cost your papa and mamma no more."

"Well, then—then—then I guess we'd bettei talk about something else," said Budge, "an' go 'long froo the woods instead of in the road. Oh—h—h!" continued Budge, kicking through some grass under the chestnut-trees by the roadside, "here's a chestnut! Is it chestnut-time again already?"

"Oh, no, that's one of last year's nuts," said Mrs. Burton.

"H'm!" exclaimed Budge; "I ought to have known that; it's dreadfully old-fashioned."

"Old-fashioned!" exclaimed Mrs. Burton.

"Why, yes; it's full of wrinkles, don't you see? like the face of Mrs. Paynter, an' you say *she's* old-fashioned."

"Aunt Alice," said Toddie, "birch-trees izh the only kind that wearzsh Sunday clothes, ain't they? Theyzh always all in white, like me and Budgie, when they goes to Sunday-school. Gwacious!" exclaimed Toddie, as he leaned against one of the birches and examined its outer garments. "Thezh Sunday trees are awful funny—thish one is singin' a song! Dzust come—hark!"

Though somewhat startled at the range of Toddie's imagination, and wondering what incentive it had on the present occasion, Mrs. Burton approached the tree, and solved the mystery by hearing the breeze sighing softly through the branches. Then she told Toddie what caused the sound, and the young man replied: "Oh! Then it's the Lord come down to sing in it 'cauzh it's got Sunday clothes on. Thatsh it, izhn't it?"

"Oh, no, Toddie; the wind is only the wind," said Mrs. Burton.

"Why, *I* always fought it wazh the Lord a-talkin' when the wind blowed. I guesh somebody tolded me so 'cauzh I fought that before I had many uvver finks."

Up the mountain-road leisurely sauntered Mrs. Burton, while her nephews examined every large stone, boulder, tree and hole in the ground. This passion for investigation was finally rewarded, for, as Toddie poked a stick into a hole at the root of a tree, a little snake came out, and seemed disposed to defend his domicile.

Toddie ran shrieking to his aunt, while Budge belabored the reptile vigorously with his own stick until it was dead.

"Ah—h—h—h!" screamed Toddie. "The hateful fing! Why don't snakesh come an' offer little boysh apples, like that one did in Adam's garden, 'stead of scarin' 'em most to deff?"

"Because snakes don't like little boys to bother them," said Mrs. Burton, trying to comfort the frightened child.

"If he would only teach me to run along the ground on my tummuk like *he* does, I wouldn't care," said Toddie. "Why don't he get dirty when he runs? See how clean an' white he is along the bottomest side of him. I wiss we'd asked him how he keeps so clean 'fore Budgie killed him."

"Why, snakes can't talk, Toddie!" said Mrs. Burton.

"Can't they?" asked Toddie. "That garden-snake did."

"*He* was somebody else—Satan was in him," said Mrs. Burton.

"Did he get inside of the snake so's to play in the dust wifout gettin' his clothes dyty?" asked Toddie.

"No. He did it to make trouble," said Mrs. Burton.

"Shouldn't fink he'd *want* to make any crubble," said Toddie, "when he could have such fun wrigglin' around!"

The top of the hill was gained at last, and, with a long-drawn "Oh!" both boys sat down upon stones and gazed in delight at the extended scene before them. Budge at last broke the silence by asking:

"Aunt Alice, don't you s'pose our friends up in heaven, is lookin' at all these towns, an' hills, an' rivers an' things, just like we are?"

"Very likely, dear," said Mrs. Burton.

"Well, then, they can see a good deal further than we can. Do our spirits have new eyes put in 'em when they get up to heaven?"

"I don't know how that is," said Mrs. Burton. "Perhaps they only have their sight made better."

"Why, does spirits take their old eyes wif 'em to hebben, an' leave all the rest part of 'em in the deader?" asked Toddie.

Mrs. Burton realized that she had been too hasty in assuming knowledge of spiritual physiognomy, and she endeavored to retract by saying:

"Spiritual eyes and bodily eyes are different."

"Does dust and choo-choo cinders ever get into spirit-eyes, an' make little boy andzels cry, and growed-up andzels say swear wordsh?" asked Toddie.

"Certainly not," said Mrs. Burton. "There's no crying or swearing in heaven."

"Then what does angels do with the water that comes in their eyes when they hear music that makes 'em feel as if wind was blowin' froo 'em?" asked Budge.

Mrs. Burton endeavored to change the subject of conversation to one with which she was more familiar, by asking him if he knew that there were hills a hundred times as high as Hawksnest Rock.

"Goodness, no!" exclaimed the child. "Why, I should think you could look right *into* heaven from the tops of them; can't you?"

"No," said Mrs. Burton, with some impatience at the result of her attempt. "Besides, their tops are covered with snow all the time, and nobody can get up to them."

"Then the little boy andzels can play snowball on 'em

wifout no cross man's comin' up an' sayin', 'Don't!'" said Toddie.

Mrs. Burton tried again:

"Just see how high that bird is flying," said she, pointing to a hawk who was soaring far above the hill.

"Yes," said Budge. "*He* can go up into heaven whenever he wants to, can't he, 'cause he's got wings. I don't know why birds have got wings and little boys haven't."

"Little boys are already hard enough to find when they're wanted," said Mrs. Burton. "If they had wings they'd always be out of sight. But what makes you little boys talk so much about heaven to-day?"

"Oh, 'cause we're up so much closer to it, I suppose," said Budge, "when we're on a high hill like this."

"Don't you think it must be nearly lunch-time?" asked Mrs. Burton, using, in despair, the argument which has seldom failed with healthy children.

"Certainly," said Budge. "I always do. Come on, Tod. Let's go the shortest way."

The shortest way was by numerous short cuts, with which the boys seemed perfectly acquainted. One of these, however, was by a very steep incline, and Budge, perhaps snuffing the lunch afar off, descended so rapidly that he lost his balance, fell forward, tried to recover himself, failed, and slipped rapidly through a narrow path which finally ended in a gutter traversing it.

"Ow!" remarked the young man as he picked himself up, and relieved himself of a mouthful of mud. "Did you see my back come up an' me walk down the mountain on my mouth? I think a snake would be ashamed of himself to see how easy it was. I didn't try a bit—I just went slip, slop, bunk! to the bottom."

"An' you didn't get scolded for dytyin' your clothes, either," said Toddie. "Let's sing 'Gloly, gloly, halle-helyah.'"

The subject of dirt upon juvenile raiment began to trouble the mind of Mrs. Burton. Could it be possible that children had a natural right to dirtier clothing than adults, and without incurring special blame? Was dirtiness sinful? Well, yes—that is, it was disgusting, and whatever was disgusting was worse in the eyes of Mrs. Burton than what was sinful. *Could* children be as neat as adults? Had they either the requisite sense, perception or the acquired habit of carefulness? Again Mrs. Burton went into a study of the brownest description, while the children improved these moments of preoccupation to do all sorts of things which would have seemed dreadful to their aunt, but were delightful to themselves. At length, however, they reached the Burton lunch-table, and managed a series of rapid disappearances for whatever was upon it.

"Aunt Alice," said Budge, after finishing his meal,

"What are you going to do to make us happy this afternoon?"

"I think," said Mrs. Burton, "I shall allow you to amuse yourselves. I shall be quite busy superintending the baking. Our cook has only lately come to us, you know, and she may need some help from me."

"I fought bakin's wazh alwayzh in mornin's?" remarked Toddie. "*My* mamma says that only lazy peoplesh bakesh in afternoonzh."

"The cook was too busily engaged otherwise this morning, Toddie," said Mrs. Burton. "Besides, people bake mornings because they are compelled to; for, when they put bread to rise overnight, they *must* bake in the morning. But there is a new kind of yeast now that lets us make our bread whenever we want to, within a couple of hours from the time of beginning."

"Do you know, Aunt Alice," said Budge, "that *we* can bake? We can—real nice. We've helped mamma make pies an' cakes lots of times, only hers are big ones an' ours are baby ones."

"I suppose I am to construe that remark as a hint that you would like to help *me?*" said Mrs. Burton. "If you will do only what you are told, you may go to the kitchen with me; but listen—the moment you give the cook or me the least bit of trouble, out you shall go."

"Oh, goody, goody!" shouted Toddie. "An' can we

have tea-parties on the kitchen-table as fast as we bake our fings?"

"I suppose so," said Mrs. Burton.

"Come on, come on!" exclaimed Toddie. "My hands won't be still a bittie, I wants to work so much. How many kindsh of pies is you goin' to make?"

"None at all," said Mrs. Burton.

"Gwacious!" exclaimed Toddie. "I shouldn't fink you'd call it bakin'-day then. Izhn't you goin' to make noffin' but ole nasty bread?"

"Perhaps I can find a way for you to make a little cake—some buns, say," remarked Mrs. Burton, relenting.

"Well, that would be *kind* o' bakin'-day like; but my hands is gettin' still again awful fasht."

Mrs. Burton led the way to the kitchen, and the preparation of the staff of life was begun by the new cook, with such assistance as could be rendered by a small boy wedged closely under each elbow, and two inquiring faces hanging over the very edge of the bread-pan.

"*That* don't look very cakey," remarked Budge. "She ain't put any powder into it."

"This kind of bread needs no powder," said Mrs. Burton. "Baking-powders are used only in tea-biscuit."

"When tea-biscuits goes in the oven they is little bits of flat fings," remarked Toddie—"theysh little bits of flat fings, but when they comes out they's awful big an' fat. What *makes* 'em bake big?"

"That's what the powder is put in for," said Mrs. Burton. "They'd be little hard, tasteless things if it weren't for the powder. Bridget, just work some sweetening with a little of the dough, so the boys can have some buns."

Both boys escorted the cook to the pantry for sugar, and back again to the table, and got their noses as nearly as possible under the roller with which the sugar was crushed, and they superintended the operation of working it into the dough, and then Mrs. Burton found some very small pans in the center of which the boys put single buns which they were themselves allowed to shape. A happy inspiration came to Mrs. Burton; she brought a few raisins from the pantry and placed one upon the centre of each tiny bun as it was made, and was rewarded by a dual shriek of delight.

"Stop, Toddie!" exclaimed Mrs. Burton, suddenly noticing that Toddie was shaping his dough by rolling it vigorously between his hands, as little boys treat clay while attempting to make marbles. "If you press your dough as hard as that, you may feel certain that it will never bake light in the world."

"You mean the hot won't make it grow big?" asked Toddie.

"Yes."

"Thatzh too baddy—it's *awful* too baddy," said Toddie. "Then there won't be as much of 'em to eat. *Tell* you what—put some powder in it to help the uvver swelly stuff."

"I'm afraid that won't do any good," said Mrs. Burton.

"Might *try* it," suggested Toddie. Ah—h—h—Budgie's makin' some of my buns baldheaded!"

"What on earth *do* you mean?" asked Mrs. Burton.

"He's takin' the raisins off of the tops of 'em, an' that makes 'em baldheaded."

"I was only keepin' 'em from lookin' all alike," explained Budge, hastily putting the raisins where they could not be affected by any future proceedings. "Don't you see, Toddie, you'll have *two* kinds of buns now?"

"Don't *want* two kindsh," cried Toddie. "I'ze a good mind to cut you open an' take them heads back again."

Budge was reproved by his aunt, and Toddie was pacified by the removal of raisins from his brother's buns to his own. Then some of the little pans were placed in the vacant space in the oven, and during the next fifteen minutes Mrs. Burton was implored at least twenty times to see if they weren't almost done. When, finally baked, Toddie's were as small as bullets and about as hard.

"Put some powder in the rest of them," pleaded Toddie.

"I'm sure it wouldn't do the slightest bit of good," said Mrs. Burton.

Further entreaties led to a conflict between will and authority, after which Toddie sulked and finally disappeared, carrying one of his precious pans with him. When, after a few moments he returned the baking was done, and the oven-door was open.

"I'zhe a-goin' to bake this uvver one *any* how," said Toddie, putting the single remaining pan into the oven and closing the door. "Say, Aunt Alice," he continued, his good-nature returning. "Now fix that tea-party we was goin' to have wif our own fings. *You* can come to the table wif us if you want to."

"Only don't you think she ought to bring somethin' with her?" asked Budge. "That's the way little boys' tea-parties out of doors always are."

Mrs. Burton herself rendered a satisfactory decision upon this question by making a small pitcher of lemonade; the table was drawn as near the door as possible, to avoid the heat of the room; Budge escorted his aunt to the seat of honor, and, when all were seated, he asked:

"Do you think these is enough things to ask a blessin' over? Sometimes we do it, an' sometimes we don't, 'cordin' to how much we've got."

Mrs. Burton rapidly framed a small explanatory lecture on the principle underlying the custom of grace at meals;

but, whatever may have been its merits, the boys never had an opportunity of judging, for suddenly a loud report, like the shot of a gun, startled the party, a piece of the stove flew violently across the room and broke against the wall, the stove-lids shivered violently and the doors fell open, the poker, which had lain on the stove, danced frantically, and a small pan of some sort of fat—such as some cooks have an insane fancy to be always doing something with, but never do it—was shaken over, and its burning contents began to diffuse a sickening odor. The cook dropped upon her knees and crossed herself; the party arose, Budge roaring, Toddie screaming, and Mrs. Burton very pale, while the cook remarked:

"Holy Mudther! The wather-back's busted!"

Mrs. Burton disengaged herself from her tightly-clinging nephews, and approached the range cautiously. There was no sign of water, and the back of the range was undisturbed; even the fire was not disarranged.

"It isn't the water-back," said Mrs. Burton, "nor the fire. What *could* it have been?"

"An' I belave, mum," said the cook, "that 'twas the dhivil, savin' yer prisince; an', saints presarve us! I've heerd at home as how he hated these new ways of cookin', because dhere was no foire place for him to sit in the corner of, bad luck to him! It was the dhivil, sure, mum," repeated the cook, crossing herself again. "Did iver ye schmell the loike av that?"

Mrs. Burton snuffed the air, and, sure enough, in spite of the loathsome odor of burning grease, she detected a strong sulphurous smell.

"An' he went and tookted my last bun wif him, too," complained Toddie, who had been cautiously approaching the oven in which he had placed his pan. "*Bad* ole debbil! I fought he didn't have noffin but roasted people at hizh tea-parties!"

The whole party was too much agitated and mystified to pursue their investigations further. The fire was allowed to die out, Mrs. Burton hurried up-stairs and to the front of the house with the children, while the cook craved and received permission to make an immediate call upon her spiritual adviser.

Mr. Burton, on his way home, was met by his wife and nephews, and heard a tale which had now reached blood-curdling proportions. His descent to the scene of the disaster was reluctantly consented to by his wife; but he was unable to discover the cause of the accident, and he succeeded in getting his hands most shockingly dirty. He hurried to his bedchamber to wash them, and a moment after he roared from the head of the stairs: "Boys, which of you have been up here to-day?"

There was no response for a moment; then Budge shouted: "Not me."

Mrs. Burton looked inquiringly at Toddie, noting which,

the young gentleman averted his eyes. Then Mı. Burton hurried down-stairs, looked at both boys and asked: "What did you meddle with my powder-flask for, Toddie?"

"Why—why—why," stammered Toddie, "Aunt Alice wouldn't put no powder in my buns to make 'em light after I rolled 'em heavy—said 'twouldn't do 'em no good. But my papa says 'tain't never no harm to try, so I dzust wented and gotted some powder out of your brass bottle that's hangin' on your gun, and I didn't say nuffin' to nobody, 'cauzh I wanted to s'prise 'em. An' while I was waitin' for it to get done bad ole debbıl came an' hookted it. Guesh it must have been real good else he wouldn't have tookted it, 'cauzh he's such a smart fief he can steal the nicest fings he wantsh—whole cake-shop windows full."

"How did you mix it with the dough?—how much did you take?" demanded Mrs. Burton.

"Didn't mixsh it at all," said Toddie; "dzush pourded it on the pan azh full azh I could. You'd fink I'd *have* to if you tried to eat one of my buns that didn't have no powder in. Gwacious! *wasn't* they hard? I couldn't bite 'em a bit—I dzust had to swallow 'em whole."

"Umph?" growled Mr. Burton. "And do you know who the devil—the *little* devil was that——"

"Harry!" remonstrated Mrs. Burton.

"Well, my dear, the truth appears to be just this: your nephew——"

"*Your* nephew, Mr. Burton!"

"Well, my—*our* nephew, put into the oven this afternoon about enough of gunpowder to charge a six-pounder shell, and the heat gradually became too much for it."

Toddie had listened to this conversation with an air of anxious inquiry, and at last timidly asked:

"Wazhn't it the right kind of powder? I fought it wazh, 'cauzh it makes everyfing else light when it goezh off."

"Do you suppose your method of training will ever prevail against that boy's logic, my dear?" asked Mr. Burton. "And if it won't, what will?"

"I won't put so much in nexsht time," said Toddie "'cauzh 'tain't no good to try a fing an' then have the tryin' stuff go an' take the fing all away from you an' get so mad as to break stoves to bits an' scare little boysh an' Aunt Alishes most to deff."

CHAPTER IX.

"W!—Ow!—Ow!" was the reveille of the Burton family on the next morning, and it was sounded from the room of the juvenile guests.

"Another fight, I suppose," grunted Mr. Burton, in his own room "and, as I'm dressed, I might as well go see which one was whipped and which ought to be."

Arrived at his nephews' room, Mr. Burton found Toddie curled up in the middle of the bed sound asleep, and his brother with his eyes shut, but wriggling restlessly.

"What's the matter, Budge?" asked Mr. Burton.

"My side hurts—where—I—bunked it stoppin' in the gutter when I slid down the mountain," drawled Budge. "An' the hard part of the bed comes up to it an' hurts it. As soon as I find a soft part of the bed, the hard part begins to come up through it an' hurts me."

"Well, suppose you were to turn over and lie on your other side!" suggested Mr. Burton.

"I—why—I—then I——" stammered Budge, arising slowly and rubbing his eyes, "then I wouldn't have any soft parts to look for, an' I wouldn't have anything to do."

"Oh, no," muttered Mr. Burton, turning abruptly and quitting the room. "The faculty of hugging misery isn't born in people—not at all. I'll have to tell this to our parson; a lot of good people that need it might get a sound thrashing then over somebody else's shoulders."

At the breakfast-table Budge ate quietly, but with characteristic American industry; finally he remarked:

"Aunt Alice, too much tea isn't good for people, is it?"

"Oh, no," said Mrs. Burton, "it's very bad."

"And," continued Budge, "one cup is enough for pretty much anybody, isn't it?"

"I think so," said Mrs. Burton.

"But sometimes my papa drinks three or four," said Budge.

"That must be when he has a headache, then," said the lady.

"Oh, yes—'tis," assented Budge. "People *need* more then, don't they?"

"Yes, indeed," said Mrs. Burton.

"Well, don't you think a sideache is as bad as a headache?" asked Budge.

Mrs. Burton guessed the sequel, but refrained from replying

"An' *awful* sideache," continued Budge, "where a little boy's side has been bumped real hard by a great big mountain's side?"

Mrs. Burton bit her upper-lip, and reached for Budge's emptied mug, which the young man accommodatingly pushed toward her, exclaiming as he did so:

"An' I think when it's a little boy that's got to drink it 'cause he's sick, there ought to be lots and lots of sugar in it, to keep the tea from bein' too strong."

Budge's mug was filled according to his liking. Mr. Burton's eyes dancing over it so busily that they could not stop when Mrs. Burton's accidentally detected them. A few moments of adult silence was the natural result, and the boys improved the opportunity to disappear without being questioned, after which Mr. Burton, starting for the city, gave shortly the monosyllable "No!" in reply to the question whether he should bring anything home.

Mrs. Burton found herself soon in the depths of another inspection of her career as a manager of children, and began to realize that she was as faulty in being too indulgent as she was in being too severe. Recalling the many smart tricks of the children to overcome her rules, she could not remember a single one at which they had not succeeded, and the realization of this was as mortifying to her sense of duty as it was to her pride. To be firm when her sense of humor was touched was a phase of ability of which she found herself to be as destitute as people usually are, but the existence of such a failing she had never even imagined before, and it doubled her sense of responsibility and—humility. But the latter quality soon was lost in one which comes so much more naturally and is always so finely and fully developed—pride. What wouldn't she have given to have that breakfast scene to manage again? To think that she, who had in every other department of life discerned sly attempts afar off and successfully circumvented them, should have been steadily outwitted by two very small boys! Oh, for just one more attempt by either of them! Mrs. Burton instinctively bit her lip until pain caused her to stop. Upon this, at any rate, she was determined: she would not only prevent her nephews from accomplishing their artfully-laid purposes, but she would explain to them how dishonest such attempts were, and endeavor to shame them into perfect ingenuousness.

At this instant the sound of a wordy altercation, momentarily growing livelier, floated up from the kitchen-windows, and Mrs. Burton started to act as arbitrator absolute.

"We *want* it—*that's* why," was heard from Budge as Mrs. Burton entered the kitchen.

"What, what?" asked the mistress (titular) of the house.

"Why," said Budge, his face lighting with the anticipation of assistance close at hand, "we've found a big nest full of eggs in the grass a good way off, an' we want to boil 'em an' eat 'em, an' I've asked Bridget over an over again for a pail to boil 'em in, an' all she says is 'Niver a bit.'"

"Which she is perfectly right in doing," said Mrs. Burton, "when, as I assume from what I overheard as I came in, you did not tell her what you wanted of the pail."

"Well," said Budge, "how could I help it? I couldn't keep rememberin' what you said to Uncle Harry the other evening, that you had the most utter contempt for people that always wanted to know about other people's business. I don't know what 'utter contempt' means, but I thought from the way you said it you meant folks who were always asking questions about what other folks was doing."

Mrs. Burton hastily took a small pail from a shelf, handed it to Budge, and said, "Take it!" while the cook remarked, "Thrue for ye, mum," and Budge walked off with his pail, and Mrs. Burton, recollecting her good resolutions, retired to her own chamber and wept despairingly. The idea of letting two small children eat a lot of eggs between meals! No one knew where they were or how many eggs they had; they probably had a fire built somewhere in which least of all a fire should be, and what damage they were threatening to property and life only

Heaven knew. She wished herself within the councils of Heaven, she committed a dozen frightful heresies while she wondered, but came back by necessity to the Christian virtue of resignation, for how to find her nephews would have puzzled a head more experienced than her own in the ways of small boys.

Mrs. Burton's morning was spent in vague attempts to do something, and it was with sincere satisfaction that she finally beheld her two nephews approaching by a road that led through woods and fields. The borrowed pail was not visible anywhere about them, but Mrs. Burton did not notice its absence. Toddie dropped dejectedly upon a large stone in the backyard, and Budge sauntered into the sitting-room with the air of a man of the world who had squeezed life's orange and found it juiceless.

"You're safely back, are you?" asked Mrs. Burton, anxious to know what had happened, but fearing to speak too pointedly."

"Oh, yes, we're *back*," said Budge; "but that don't do us any good."

"Why, what can be the matter with my dear little Budge?" exclaimed Mrs. Burton.

"A good deal," said Budge. "There's some awful funny things in this world, Aunt Alice, an' they ain't nice either."

"Tell me all about them, dear!" said Mrs. Burton.

"Well," said Budge, "I was awful disappointed to-day. We found sixteen eggs in a nest, an' I came all the way home to get somethin' to cook 'em in, an' I carried some salt an' pepper with me to help 'em taste nice, an' when we cooked 'em, what do you think? There was a little chicken inside of each of 'em."

"Dis—gusting!" exclaimed Mrs. Burton with a shudder.

"I know it is," said Budge; "an' I guess *you'd* have thought so more yet if you'd been there when we opened 'em. You know how nice eggs smell when you open 'em? Well, those eggs didn't even smell good a bit."

"Let's talk of something else, Budge," said Mrs. Burton, instinctively raising her handkerchief to her nose.

"But I ain't through yet," said Budge. "I want to know why the little chickens didn't come out of their shells to their mamma, instead of waitin' to bother *us?*"

"Because you scared their mamma away from them, I uppose, when you found the nest," said Mrs. Burton.

"Why, no we didn't," said Budge. "She just *went* away. We said, 'Chick, chick, chick!' to her, an' she just ran around an' cackled, so we s'posed she'd got through with the nest, an' we took what was in it to keep them from bein' spoiled. Papa says eggs always spoil when they lie out in the sunshine. What do you s'pose that poor hen-mamma 'll think when she comes walkin' along that way some day, an' sees all her dear little children lyin' around mussed up in the grass?"

"She will probably think that some meddlesome little boys have been along that way, an' haven't cared for anything or anybody but themselves," said Mrs. Burton.

Budge looked quickly up into his aunt's face; but finding neither humor nor sympathy there, he sighed deeply, and started to rejoin his brother.

"Budge!" said Mrs. Burton.

The young man arrested his steps, and looked back inquiringly.

"When you want anything," said the lady, "as, foı instance, an extra cup of tea this morning, or that paıl to boil eggs in, the proper way to do is to ask for it honestly, and if some grown person refuses to give it to you, you should be satisfied with the reasons they give, and make no trouble about it. You ought to love what is right so much that you will be ashamed to get around it in some underhand way."

"Why, 'tain't any underhand way to say just what I think, is it?" asked Budge. "Papa says folks ought always to be honest, an' say just exactly what they mean. An' I'm sure I always do it, but I like to say things the way that I think folks listen to 'em best. Ain't that the way *you* do?"

Mrs. Burton could not say no, and would not say yes, so she walked off and left her nephew master of the field, from which he himself soon retired, in response to repeated shouts of "Bud—gie!" from his brother.

"Oh, Budge!" exclaimed Toddie, as the former rejoined him, "I'zhe *got* him! oh, I'zhe *got* him! Ain't you glad?"

"Who you got?" asked Budge, not inclined to be glad without sufficient cause.

"Got Terry," exclaimed Toddie. "Got doggie Terry."

"Ow!" shouted Budge, clapping his hands and dancing about, 'that's the nicest thing I ever heard of! Just *won't* we have fun! How'd you catch him?"

"Why, he was asleep, and I djust tied a skring to his collar, and tied the uvver end to a little tree, an' there he is. See him?"

The brothers moved toward the dog, and the doomed animal, after one frantic tug at his bonds, recognized the inevitable, and shrank whimperingly against the tree.

"Poor doggie's sick, Tod," said Budge. We'll have to play doctor to him an' make him well. *I* think he ought to go to bed, don't you?"

"Yesh," said Toddie, "an' have a nightgown on, like we do when we're sick."

"That's so," said Budge. "You run and get yours for him. He needs a pretty little one, you know. I guess you'd better take off your shoes, so's not to disturb Aunt Alice."

Toddie cast his shoes and vanished, returning speedily with a robe, in which the dog Terry, not without considerable remonstrance, was soon enveloped, after which Budge lifted him tenderly in his arms, saying:

"His nightgown hangs down an awful lot, I think. I guess we'd better pin up the bottom part, like nurse did for the sister baby the other day.

"Hazhn't got no pins." said Toddie.

"Then we'll *tie* it up with a string. Besides, when it's tied up he can't get his feets out an' forget what a poor little sick doggie he is."

In another moment the superabundant skirts were fold-up and tied tightly around the poor animal's body, while Toddie, who was having great trouble to hold the stout little dog, exclaimed:

"My! the *front* end is *awful* well! See how it keeps not keepin' still. I don't fink his nightgown-collar looksh very nysh, does *you?*"

"No," said Budge, "an' he'll go right out of it if we don't make it look nice. I'll put a string around that, too. There! I want to know if anybody ever saw a lovelier-lookin' sick dog than that! Where'll we put him to bed now?"

"Let's wock him," suggested Toddie, "that's what *we* likes when we's sick."

"Then we've got to take him in the house, I guess," said Budge, "'cause there ain't anyway of makin' believe rockin'-chair. Come on!"

Quietly the couple sneaked into the house and up to their room. Then Budge resigned his precious burden for a moment to Toddie's care, while he went in search of a rocking-chair, with which he shortly returned.

"There!" said he, taking the invalid and seating himself, "that is something *like* playin' doctor. But I wonder what kind of medicine he ought to have—pills or powders?"

"Or runney stuff out of a bottle?" suggested Toddie.

"*That's* so," said Budge. "I guess it 'pends on what kind of medicine we've got. We might make him some nice pills out of soap."

"*I* know," said Toddie, going into the closet and bringing from a corner an old winter cloak trimmed with beads and picking some of the beads from it, "*these* is sp'endid for pills—*I* took some of 'em the uvver day, when I wazh playin' doctor an' sick boy, too, an' they didn't taste bad a bit."

"All right," said Budge; "pick us some off."

This order was obeyed, and soon the jet beads were being carefully dropped, one by one, down the dog's throat, Budge opening the animal's mouth with one finger, as he had seen his father do. Finally, however, the dog's jaws closed tightly.

"*I* want to make him well," said Toddie. "I ain't doctored him a bit yet."

"Well, I scarcely know what you can do for him," said Budge, "for he won't take any more pills. Perhaps there's a sore place on his head somewhere that you might put a stickin'-plaster on. But you haven't got any plaster. Oh, *I'll* tell you what—you can get a postage-stamp out of Uncle Harry's desk—*that'll* do for a stickin'-plaster first rate."

"I wantsh to wock him," said Toddie, "'sides doctorin' him."

"I'm 'fraid 'twon't be best to move him just now," said Budge, scanning the face of the patient with considerable solicitude.

"*I* tell you what, then," said Toddie, with the air of a man to whom had come a direct inspiration, "let's stop makin' believe for a minute, until I get hold of him—*then* he can be made back into a sick boy again."

"All right," said Budge, though evidently convinced against his will; "I s'pose I've got to, so that all the doctors get a chance at him. But say, papa says mixin' doctors kills sick folks—don't you think we'd better talk it all over again? 'Twould be dreadful if Uncle Harry's dear little dog was made dead, you know."

"Aw wight," said Toddie, "an' I'll hold him while we talk about it—I won't give him a single bittie of medshin till we know dzust what he ought to have."

"Mebbe different people's arms makes a difference to sick folks," suggested Budge, holding the patient still more tenderly, and oblivious to Toddie's outstretched arms. "Don't you know mamma used to say about Phillie that it made all the difference in the world who held him? —that medicine seemed to stop goin' around in his dear little bones and muscles to make 'em well when some folks got hold of him? An' don't you know how he used to yowl when *you* came up to him?"

"Thatsh 'cauzh I used to put my fingers in his eyes to see what the bright part was made of. Never done that to Terry—couldn't never catch him to do it. Dzust see how sad he looks at you! I fink his eyes is a-sayin', 'Oh, I'll *die* if that dear Doctor Toddie don't nurse me!' I shouldn't fink you could be so dreadful cruel, Budgie."

Budge reluctantly relinquished his precious burden, and Toddie bestowed upon the patient a squeeze so affectionate that the poor dog howled piteously, and struggled to free himself.

"There!" said Budge, "what did I tell you? You're the kind of folks that don't agree with him, you see."

"'Tain't me," said Toddie. "I guesh it's the medshin takin' effec'. Them beads—pills, I mean—can't get into his bonesh an' mushels wifout skwatchin' them."

"I s'pect that's 'cause we forgot to give 'em to him in something nice, like papa gives us *our* medicine!"

"Letsh give him somefin' nysh *now*, then," said Toddie "Mebbe it can find the medshin, an' they'll go along nysh togevver, dzust like two little budders."

"All right," said Budge. "What'll it be?"

"Cake," suggested Toddie.

"Who'll ask Aunt Alice for it?" asked Budge. "I guess *you'd* better; I did last time we wanted cake. Anyhow, that is, I was gettin' it without askin', an' promised her I'd always ask after that."

"Then you ought to begin right skraight away," said Toddie, "elsh mebbe you'd forget. *I* know what you wantsh; you wantsh me to ask, so's you can get poor sick baby again while I go."

"Well," said Budge, somewhat abashed, "I suppose I'll have to."

Budge departed, and returned within two or three minutes with a large piece of fruit-cake and a radiant countenance.

"I tell you, Tod, just don't folks get paid for bein' good! I was goin' down to ask Aunt Alice, just as good as could be, and then I couldn't find her anywhere in the house, so there wasn't anything to do but go get the cake myself. I don't b'leeve we'd have got such a big piece, either, if she'd been there. Now I know what that big thing on the Sunday-school wall means—'Virtue is its own reward.'"

"Gwacious Peter!" exclaimed Toddie, extending his hand for the cake. "We dassent give him all *that*—'twould make him dream *dreadful* fings" Here Toddie put the cake to the dog's mouth, and the animal eagerly bit at it. "Goodnesh! I forgot that dogs could open moufs bigger than babies. I fink he's got more now than's goin' to agree wif him. G'way!" continued Toddie, as the dog again snapped at the cake. "We'ze got to put this where he can't see it, 'less he'll be cryin' for it all the time!"

And, with admirable quickness of resource, Toddie hastily crowded a large portion of the remainder into his own mouth,

"Oh—h—h!" exclaimed Budge, moving hastily to the rescue of the remainder of the cake, "*you* ain't took no medicine, an' you'll dream of more cows (the night-*mare* of the Lawrences was always a cow) than you ever saw. "Give me it!"

"Um—m—m—ugh—mow—moo—um—guh!" mumbled Toddie, with difficulty, as he tightened his grasp on the remainder of the cake!"

"Oh, *give* it to me, Tod," pleaded Budge. "I'll eat it and then I'll dream 'bout the same cows that you do; don't you know how often you wish I'd dream the same things as you do, an' get mad 'cause I don't?"

Toddie indulged in some terrific final gulps, and then coughed violently, but at last said:

"It's drefful to dream about cows, an' I loves you cauzh you's my dee budder Budgie, an' I don't want you to djeam drefful fings." Here Toddie hastily crammed most of the remainder of the cake into his mouth, and handed the rest to his brother, saying: "That'll make—you—djeam 'bout—two or—free cows, an' so it'll let you get into the djeam wifout havin' suts drefful times as I'zh got to."

Budge might perhaps have recognized in fitting terms this evidence of brotherly forethought, but his mouth found other occupation for a moment. Meanwhile the unfortunate patient was wriggling and whimpering; finally, by a desperate effort, he freed himself from Toddie's embrace and fell upon the floor where he rolled frantically about with many contortions and howls.

"Oh, he's got a convulsion—I guess he must be havin' a stomach-toof come!" said Budge; "what *can* we do?"

"Pallygollic," suggested Toddie.

"We ain't got none," said Budge. "*Tell* you what, let's make b'lieve he's a dog a minute, an' throw water on him—that's what they do to dogs in fits."

"Then we'd get Aunt Alice's nice carpet all wetty," said Toddie. "Let's put him in the baff-tub."

"That's just the thing," said Budge, picking up the animal, while Toddie ran before and turned on the water. The dog was dropped into the tub, where he naturally re-

"Say, Tod, its *hot* water they set babies in when the toofs bother 'em
—we'll make b'lieve he's a baby again, an' turn on

doubled his exertions to free himself, noting which, Budge remarked :

"Say, Tod, it's *hot* water they set babies in when the toofs bother 'em—we'll make b'leeve he's a baby again, an' turn on t'other faucet."

Toddie quickly opened the hot water faucet, and the poor animal recognizing his inability to release himself, began at about the same time to accept the inevitable.

"There—he's gettin' better," said Budge, observing the animal with professional closeness. "I guess he can come out now. Ow, oh !—that water's *awful* hot ! How *are* we goin' to get him out ?"

Toddie leaned over the edge of the tub and seized the dog by the head. The animal struggled violently ; Toddie redoubled his exertions and devoted his mind to the task. Suddenly he lost his balance and tumbled headlong into the tub himself, from which he speedily scrambled, howling violently, while Budge snatched the animal's head and landed him, too, upon the bath-room floor.

"Oh, de—oh !" cried Toddie.

"Does it hurt you *awful*, dear little brother ?" asked Budge, tenderly.

"No," said Toddie. "The hurtz'h gone off me, but—*oh*, dear !—I gotted a lot of water in my mouf, an' it washed out all the taste of the cake. I fink it's too good for nuffin' mean for anyfing."

"Well, I guess you'd better sit out in the sun an' dry yourself," said Budge, "and change the poor doggie's clothes for him."

"Wantsh *my* clozhezsh tshanged," sobbed Toddie.

"Come on then," said Budge, leading the way back to his own room, and dragging the bundle of wet dog behind him. There!" said he, shutting the door, "you dress yourself, and I'll fix the dog."

Carefully untying the strings that confined the animal, but taking the precaution to tie one to Terry's collar, and the other end to a chair, Budge removed the nightgown, brought a brush, comb, and bottle of cologne from his aunt's room, and he began to brush the dog's coat, pouring on cologne without stint.

The animal was too grateful to be upon his feet again to offer any serious remonstrance, and the toilet operations continued until, suddenly, Budge poured considerable cologne upon his head. The liquid found its way to Terry's eyes, and the spirits which composed so much of it immediately put the poor brute into such pain that he began to dash frantically about the room, dragging the light chair after him. Budge had left the door open on returning from his aunt's chamber, and through this and down the stairs, dashed Terry.

The top of the chair struck the stair-rail, and resolved itself at once into its original parts; the remainder of this average sample of American furniture flew down the stairs after the dog, and executed a rapid semicircle in air at the foot, encountering a handsome cabinet hat-rack on the way, to the severe damage of the polish on this latter. Then, still obeying the inexorable demands imposed by the string, the other end of which was attached to the dog's collar, it meandered through the parlor, leaving a leg with the piano-pedal, as a trophy for the latter of a little conflict between them—attempted to go up a chimney through the fireplace, but got only so far as the andirons, whose positions it seriously compromised—lodged between the legs of an antique table, to the complete prostration of the table itself, and the leaving of the seat of the chair among the late contents of the table—struck a jardinière, which promptly came down with a crash—flew into the dining-room, into a chair, across the table, from which it snatched a cover, with which, for a moment or two, it was seriously mixed, and finally went down the kitchen-stairs, encountering Mrs. Burton on her return from an interview with the green-grocer. As the chair was one of special lightness and exceeding cost, Mrs. Burton naturally desired to interview Terry ; but the overtasked animal had evidently formed other plans which he did not intend should be thwarted, so, with a vicious snap, he eluded her, dashed through the kitchen, and sought the shady solitude of the forest.

Intuition and experience combined to suggest to Mrs. Burton the original causes of Terry's excitement; so, waiting only a few moments, that she might be perfectly calm and righteously judicial, she started in search of the culprits. They were not in their room, though a heap of wet clothing and a general displacement of everything proved that they had been there since the chambermaid had put the room in order. A further search disclosed Toddie upon Mrs. Burton's own bed, so honestly and soundly asleep that she had not the heart to wake him. Determining then that Budge must be the sole culprit, she continued her search, and finally found the young man leaning pensively out of a window in a little observatory at the top of the house. The rustle of his aunt's dress aroused him, and bending upon her a look of most exquisite yet melancholy sensitiveness, he said:

"Aunt Alice, everybody must die, mustn't they?"

"Yes," replied Mrs. Burton, with emphasis, "and if *you* had paid the debt of nature before destroying my pretty chair, your earthly influence might have been less injurious than it has proved to be this morning."

"But, Aunt Alice," said Budge, honestly absorbed in his own thoughts, "do you see that graveyard way off yonder?—it's awful full of dead folks, ain't it?"

"Very," said Mrs. Burton, "but what they have to do with a ruined chair I confess I am unable to divine."

"Well, what I want to know," said Budge, still oblivious to everything but the question in hand, "what *I* want to know is, who's goin' to throw flowers into the last man's grave, an' who's goin' to make the hole that he's put into? What, if he should be me? I'd feel awful bothered to know what to do to be funeraled. *I* know what I'd do—I'd just pray the Lord to take me straight up to heaven like he did the good old Elijah. Say, Aunt Alice, what drawed the chariot that Elijah went to heaven in?—did those ravens do it that used to bring him his lunch?"

"I don't know," said Mrs. Burton, "but no chariot would ever have come for him at all if he had been in the habit of breaking up other people's chairs and tying the pieces to dogs."

"Why," said Budge, beginning to comprehend the drift of his aunt's remarks, "*I* didn't tie any piece of any chair to any dog. I tied *all* of Terry to a chair, an' I was bein' as nice to him as you ever was to me, an' all of a sudden he ran away with the whole of the chair You remember that story in the Bible about some bad devils goin' into a lot of pigs an' makin' 'em jump over the mountain-side into the ocean? Well, I think some of those same chaps must have got into Terry."

Mrs. Burton's faith in this demonological suggestion was not as strong as it might have been, but her wrath had been dissipated; so to escape further humiliation, she abruptly left Budge and descended to the parlor. The scene which she there beheld was one to which womanly language could not do justice, and her hurried attempts to repair the damage done were not sufficient to prevent the reawakening of her anger. And while she was still in the depths of indignant despair, her nephew, Budge, entered the room and exclaimed: "Why, Aunt Alice! how did you upset that table an' break that handsome vase of make-believe flowers?"

Mrs. Burton instinctively rose to her feet, assumed the conventional attitude of Lady Macbeth, shook her finger at Budge so menacingly that the young man fell back, while his aunt exclaimed only:

"To-morrow!"

CHAPTER X.

"THE beginning of the end," was the remark with which Mr. Burton broke a short silence at his beakfast-table, on the last day of the time for which his little visitors had been invited.

Mrs. Burton looked meek and made no reply.

"Budders," said Mr. Burton, addressing his nephews, "do you feel reconstructed?"

"Huh?" asked Budge.

"Do you feel mentally and morally reconstructed?" repeated the uncle.

"Reconwhichted?" asked Budge.

"That's an *awful* big wyde" (word), remarked Toddie, through a mouthful of oatmeal porridge. "It's like what the minister says in chych sometimes, an' makes me want to play around in the seat."

"Reconstructed—made over again," explained Mr. Burton.

"Why, no," said Budge, after looking at his hands and feeling for his stomach, as if to see if any radical physical change had taken place without his knowledge. "Maybe we're a little bigger, but we can't see ourselves when we grow."

"Don't you feel as if you wanted to see that baby sister again?" asked Mrs. Burton, endeavoring to change the subject. "Don't you want to go back to her and stay all the time?"

"*I* don't," said Toddie, "'cauzh there ain't no dog at our house, an' tryin' to catch dogs is fun 'cept when they never want to be catched at all, like Terry is such lotsh of the time."

"I mean, haven't you learned since you've been here to be a great deal better than you ever were before?" asked Mr. Burton, cruelly oblivious to his wife's evident desire.

"I guesh so," remarked Toddie. "I'zhe said more prayersh an' sung more little hymns than I ever did in all my life before. An' I ain't pulled off any more hind hoppers from grasshoppers sinsh Aunt Alice told me it wazh bad. I only pulls off *front* hoppers now. They'zh real little, you know—there's only a little bittie of them to feel hurted."

"How is it with *you*, Budge?" asked Mr. Burton. "Do you feel as if you had learned to act from different motives?"

"What's a motive?" asked Budge; "anything like a *loco*-motive? I never feel like them, 'xcept when I run pretty hard; *then* I puff like everything, only steam don't come out of me. An' then I always think there's an engine inside of me, goin' punk! punk! like everything. Papa says it's only a heart—a little bit of a boy's heart, but if that's all, I should think a big man's heart could pull a whole train of cars."

"You haven't learned to bear in mind the subject of conversation, anyhow. But have you become able to comprehend the inner significance of things?"

"Things inside of us, do you mean?" asked Budge.

"Like oatmeal porridge?" suggested Toddie.

"Have you realized that a master mind has been exerting a reformatory influence upon you?"

"Izh master-mind an' '*must* mind' the same fing?" asked Toddie. "We wasn't doin' noffin' 'cept eatin' our breksups. Don't see what we's got to mind about."

"Have you always unhesitatingly obeyed your aunt's commands, moved thereunto by a sense of her superiority by divine right?"

"Now, Harry!" exclaimed Mrs. Burton, who during all this conversation had been making mute appeals which her husband could not have resisted had he seen them, and knowing of the existence of which he had carefully kept his eyes averted from the lady's face. "If you don't stop tormenting those poor children with stupid sections of dictionary *you* shall realize my superiority by divine right, for I'll take them up-stairs and away from you."

"Only one more question, my dear," said Mr. Burton, "and I'll have done. I want only to ask the boys if they've noticed any conflicts of hereditary, and, if so, which side has triumphed?"

"I guess you are tryin' to play preacher, like Tod said," remarked Budge.

"Oh!" said Mr. Burton, blushing a little under a merry laugh from his wife. "Well, how does it affect you?"

"It makes me feel like I do in church when I wish Sunday-school time would hurry up," said Budge.

"Me too," remarked Toddie.

"You can run away and play, now," said Mr. Burton, seeing that the children's plates were empty.

The boys departed, the dog Terry apparently leading the way, yet being utterly invisible when the children reached the open air.

"You needn't have humiliated me before *them*," said Mrs. Burton, with the first pout her husband had ever seen on her face.

Mr. Burton hastened to make the *amende honorable* peculiar to the conjugal relation, and said:

"Don't fear, my dear, they didn't understand."

"Oh, didn't they?" exclaimed Mrs. Burton. "I wish all my adult friends had as quick perceptions as those boys. They may not understand big words, but tones and looks are enough for them."

"Why!" said Mr. Burton, "they scarcely looked up from their plates."

"Never mind," replied the lady, delighted at an opportunity to reassert her superiority in at least one particular. "Children—boys—are more like women than they are like men. Their unblunted sensibilities are quick; their intuition is simply angelic—would that their other qualities were also so perfect."

"I'm very sorry, then, my dear," said Mr. Burton, temporarily subjugated, "that I said a word to them, and when you are ready to kneel upon the stool of repentance I'll depart and leave you alone."

"You'll have no occasion to go," said Mrs. Burton. "I've confessed already—to them, and a single confession is enough. I rather like the operation, when, for my reward, I receive sympathy instead of sarcasm."

"Again, I ask forgiveness," said Mr. Burton; "and having made a fellow-penitent of myself, can't I have good in return for my evil, and know what a fellow-sufferer has learned from experience?"

"Just this," said Mrs. Burton; "that nobody is fit to care for children excepting the children's own parents."

Mr. Burton dropped knife and fork.

"My dear," said he, "that's better than an experience—it's a revelation. I always pronounced you a saint. Now you prove that I've always been right."

Mrs. Burton regained her pride, and with it her temporarily absent pleasantness of countenance.

"I think," she remarked, "that only one of kindred blood can comprehend an adult——"

"Unless they are modest enough to go out of themselves for a little while," suggested Mr. Burton.

Mrs. Burton opened her eyes very wide and dropped her lip a little, but recovered herself enough to finish her sentence by saying:

"And I think it ever so much harder to comprehend children, with their imperfect natures that never develop harmoniously, and that can but seldom express themselves intelligently."

"I never noticed that the boys were at a loss to express themselves when they wanted anything," said Mr. Burton.

"That sounds just like a man," said Mrs. Burton, fully herself again. "As if children had no desires and yearnings excepting for material things! What do you suppose it means when Budge sits down in a corner, goes into a brown study, and, when asked what the matter is, drawls Nothing!' in a tone that indicates that a very considerable something is puzzling his young head! What does it mean when Toddie asks his half-funny, half-pathetic questions about matters too great for his comprehension, and looks as wistful as ever after he is answered? Do you suppose they care for nothing but food and play?"

Mr. Burton felt completely humbled, and his looks evinced the nature of his feeling. At last he said:

"You are right, little woman. I wish I might have consulted you before I took the boys in hand last summer."

"And I'm very glad you didn't," said Mrs. Burton; "for—for you did a great deal better with them than you could have done if I had then been your adviser. There is some of the same blood in both of you, and you succeeded in many points where I have blundered. Oh, if I had but known it all before they came! How much I might have saved them—and myself."

Mr. Burton hastened to extend to his wife some mute sympathy.

"They're going to-day," said Mrs. Burton, finding something in her eyes that required the attention of her kerchief—"just as I've learned what I should be to them! They're angels, in spite of their pranks, and it's always so with angels' visits—one never discovers what they are until they spread their wings to depart."

"This particular pair of angels can be borrowed for an extra day, I suppose, if you desire it?" suggested Mr. Burton.

"I declare," said Mrs. Burton, "that's a brilliant idea. I'll go tell Helen that I don't think she's yet fit to have them back again."

"And I," said Mr. Burton, preparing to go to the city, "will try to persuade Tom into the same belief. I know he'll look like a man being led to execution, though."

The Burtons left the house together a few minutes later, and the boys returned very soon after. Being unable to find their aunt, they descended to the kitchen, and made a formal demand upon the cook for saucers, spoons, sugar and cream.

"An' fhot are yees up to now?" asked Bridget.

"You'll see, after you give us the things," said Budge.

"Theysh the reddisht, biggesht ones I ever saw anywhersh," remarked Toddie.

"I don't want ye to be takin' the things way off to nobody but the dhivil knows where," said Bridget. "Fhot if yees should lose one of the shpoons an' the misthress 'ud think I sthole it?"

"Oh, we won't go anywheres but 'cept under the trees in the back yard," pleaded Budge. "An' there's all the nice berries spoilin' now while you're botherin' about it. My papa says berries ought always to be eaten just when they're picked."

"Av it's only berries, I s'pose yees can have the things," muttered Bridget, bringing from a closet a small tray, and covering it with the desired articles.

"Give us another saucer, an' we'll bring you some,"

said Budge, "'cause you're nice to us. We'll need more sugar, though, if we're goin' to do that."

In the presence of flattery Bridget showed herself only a woman. She replaced the teacup of sugar with a well-filled bowl; she even put a few lumps on top of the powdered article which filled the bowl, and as the boys departed she remarked to the chambermaid that "that bye Budge is a rale gintleman. I've heard as how his father's folks came from the ould counthry, an', mark me words, Jane, they're from the Oirish nobility."

A few minutes later Mrs. Burton emerged from the sick-room of her sister-in-law. She had meant to stay but a moment, but Mrs. Lawrence's miniature had, as a special favor, been placed in Mrs. Burton's arms, and it was *so* wee and helpless, and made such funny little noises, and blinked so inquiringly, and stretched forth such a diminutive rose petal of a hand, that time had flown in apprehension, and sent the nurse to recapture the baby and vanish the visitor. And Mrs. Burton was sauntering leisurely homeward, and looking at nothing in particular, touching tenderly with the tip of her parasol the daisies and buttercups that looked up to her from the roadside, stopping even to look inquiringly upon a solitary ewe, who seemed very solicitous for the welfare of a lamb which playfully evaded her, when suddenly Mrs. Burton heard a howl, a roar, and a scream inextricably mixed. She immediately dropped all thoughts of smaller beings, for she recognized the tones of her nephews Budge and Toddie. A moment later, the noise increasing in volume all the while, both boys emerged from behind a point of woods, running rapidly, and alternately howling and clapping their hands to their mouths. Mrs. Burton ran to meet them, and exclaimed:

"Boys, do stop that dreadful noise. What *is* the matter?"

"Ow—um—oh!" screamed Budge.

"Wezh been—ow—eatin' some—some *ow*—some pieces of the bad playsh," said Toddie, "wif, oh, *oh*—cream an' sugar on 'em, but they wazh dzust as hot as if noffin' was on 'em."

"Come straight back and let aunty see about it," said Mrs. Burton, thoroughly mystified, but Budge howled and twitched away, while Toddie said:

"Wantzh papa an' mamma—theyzh had all little boy bovvers an' knowsh what to do. Wantsh to get in our ice-housh an' never go—ow—out of it."

The screaming of the children had been heard further than Mrs. Burton imagined it could be, for a sound of heavy and rapid footsteps increased behind her, and turning, she beheld the faithful Mike, Mr. Lawrence's gardener-coachman.

"Fhot is it, dharlin's?" asked Mike, looking sharply at

each boy, and picking a red speck from the front of Toddie's dress. "Murther alive! red peppers."

Mike dashed across the street, vaulted a fence, and into an inclosed bit of woodland, ran frantically about among the trees, stopped in front of one and attacked it with his knife, to the astonishment of Mrs. Burton, who imagined the man had lost his wits. A few seconds later he returned with a strip of bark, which he cut into small pieces as he ran.

"Here, ye dharlin' little dhivils," said he, cramming a piece of the bark into each boy's mouth, "chew *that* up. It's slippery elm—it'll sthop the burnin'. Don't the byes play that trick on the other byes at school often an' often, an' hasn't me sister's childher been nearly murthered by it? An' fhot ought your father do to yees for throyin' to shwally such thrash? Oh, but wouldn't I loike to foind the dhivils that put yees up to it! Who was they? Tell me, so I can sind them afther their father whose risidince is hotter than red peppers."

"How *did* you come to eat peppers?" asked Mrs. Burton, as the children escaped slowly from their pain.

"Why, a boy once told us they was strawberries," cried Budge, "an' to-day we saw a lot of them where men was spoilin' a garden to build a house, an' we asked 'em if we could have 'em, an' they said yes, an' we brought 'em all back in a piece of paper, an' didn't bite one of 'em, 'cause we wanted to eat 'em all in a little tea-party like gentle men, and the first one I chewed—*ow!* That poor rich man in the fire—I know just how he felt when he begged Abraham to have his tongue cooled with a drop of water."

"Poor old rich man didn't have *all* the fire in hizh mouf, 'spectin' that 'twazh goin' to be strawberries," sobbed Toddie.

"But there wasn't no dear old Mike to go an' get him slippery elm, either," said Budge. "Soon's we come back home to stay, Mike, I'm goin' to put dirt in the stable-pump, just to be real good about stoppin' when you tell me to."

"An' I," said Toddie, "izh goin' to make you a present all alone by myseff. I don't know yet what it'll be—I guess it'll have to be a s'prise. What would you like best—a gold watch or piece of peanut candy?"

Between two presents of value so nearly equal, Michael, the benefactor, found some difficulty in deciding, and he walked away with that application of fingers to head which is peculiar to many persons when in a quandary. Meanwhile Mrs. Burton led the children toward her own house, saying:

"What can we do to-day that can be extremely nice, little boys? Mamma expects you home to-morrow, and Aunt Alice wants to make your last day a very happy one."

"To-morrow!" exclaimed Budge, oblivious to all else

his aunt had said. "Why, I thought we were going home to-day?"

"So you were, dear," said Mrs. Burton; "but you didn't seem to be in any hurry, and I couldn't bear to let you go so soon. Did you really want to go to-day?"

"Well, I've been thinkin' about it an' countin' days till to-day ever since we've come," said Budge. "Sometimes it seemed as if I'd *burst* if I couldn't be back home again; but I tried to be real good about it, 'cause papa said 'twould be better for the sister-baby and mamma if we staid away. Sometimes, in the night-time, I've cried because I wasn't in *my* little bed."

"Why, you poor little boy," said Mrs. Burton, stopping to kiss Budge, "why didn't you tell Aunt Alice when you were so unhappy?"

"*You* couldn't do me any good," said Budge; "*nobody* could but my papa or mamma. An' then I don't like to tell what's hurtin' my heart—somethin' in my throat makes me hate to tell such things!"

"Haven't you had a pleasant time at our house? When you've not been doing whatever you liked, haven't Uncle Harry and I been trying to make you happy?"

"Oh, yes," sighed Budge. "But some folks know just what we like, and some other folks know what they want us to like; and the first some folks are my papa an' mamma, an' the other some folks are you an' Uncle Harry.

You've done some real nice things for us, though, an' I'm goin' to ask mamma to let us invite *you* to *our* house, an' then I'll show you how to take care of little boys an' make 'em happy!"

"You come to vizhit at our housh," said Toddie, "an' you can have cake between mealsh, an make mud-pies whenever you want to, no matter if youzh got your very besht clozhezh on. An' I won't ever say 'Don't!' to you one single time!"

"An' you shall have your own mamma come every day, to frolic an' cut up with you," said Budge. "I wish you had a papa—we'd have him too!"

"Aunt Alice," said Budge, "how do big folks get along without papas an' mammas?"

"I don't know, I'm sure, dear," said Mrs Burton, remembering how helpless she found herself when her husband first took her from beneath her mother's wing.

"Don't they ever have something to tell 'em to don't, an' then feel like somebody else when they find they ain't there to tell 'em to?"

"I—I suppose some do," said Mrs. Burton, recalling some periods of her own life when she longed for a confidant who should be neither lover nor friend.

"Don't you think maybe they look all around then, an' think the nicer things are the lonelier they are?" continued Budge.

"Yes, dear," replied Mrs. Burton, putting a kiss upon the young man's forehead.

"Musht be awful not to have anybody to ask for pennies when youzh lonesome an' don't know what else to do," remarked Toddie.

"An' not to have anybody hold you to keep from kind o' tumblin' to pieces when you've seen enough of everything, an' done enough of everything, an' don't know what's goin' to happen next, an' wish it wouldn't happen at all," said Budge. "Say, Aunt Alice, folks don't ever have to feel that way when they get to be angels, do they?"

"No, indeed," said Mrs. Burton.

"Well, do you think it makes folks in heaven happy to have a father—the Lord, you know—when there ain't anything to ask Him for? If they're happy the whole time, I don't see when they can think about how nice it is to have a heaven papa. Do little angels ever have to go away from home an' stay a few days, an' not see their father at all?"

"Mercy—no!" exclaimed Mrs. Burton, with a shudder. "Where *do* you get such ideas, Budge?"

"Nowhere," said the boy. "I don't get 'em at all—*they* get *me*, an' don't let go of me until I think myself most to pieces, or else get somethin' new to do that makes me forget 'em."

Mrs. Burton mentally resolved to immediately find something new for Budge to do, if only to keep him from leading her mind upon ground which, being unknown to her, she assumed must be dangerous. Her anxiety was not lessened when Toddie strayed into more active conversation.

"Aunt Alish," said he, "what does little boy angels do with their pennies when they get 'em? Ish there candy stores up in hebben, and do the folks that keeps 'em give more for a penny than they do here?"

"Pennies are of no use in heaven, Toddie," said Mrs. Burton, almost frantic to find a way of escape from the pair of literalists, yet remembering her longings of the early morning to have the boys with her, that she might find her way to their hearts and lead them into her own.

"What!—not good for anyfing?" asked Toddie. "Wouldn't it be djeadful then if I was to get to be an angel right now—there'sh sixty-four pennies in my savings bank."

"You can't carry pennies to heaven, you silly boy!" exclaimed Budge. "In a place where all the streets are made of gold, you don't suppose anybody cares for pennies, do you, Toddie? I don't s'pose you could buy a single stick of candy for less than a whole dollar bill."

"If you little boys are so fond of candy," said Mrs. Burton, in theological desperation, "we will make a lot ourselves right after lunch."

"Oh, *oh!*" exclaimed Budge. "Can common folks like us make candy?"

"Certainly," said Mrs. Burton; "but we are not common folks, Budge."

"*I* think we are," said the boy, "when I think about what lovely people candy-makers must be."

"How much will we make?" asked Toddie, "*Two* pennies' worth?"

"Oh, yes; more than two little boys can eat in a day."

"Gwacious Peter!" exclaimed Toddie, "that would be more than a whole candy-store full! Come on! Don't letsh eat any lunch at all, so's to have our tummuks all empty for the candy."

"I'll bet I can walk faster than *you* can, Aunt Alice," said Budge, tugging at his aunt with one hand and pushing her with the other.

"*I* can *run* fashter than bofe of you," shouted Toddie; "come on!"

Mrs. Burton declined both challenges, but the boys went rapidly over the course without her, and ran frantically up and down the piazza until their aunt joined them.

"What are you goin' to make it in, Aunt Alice?" shouted Budge, while his aunt was yet a hundred yards away.

"A saucepan," replied the lady.

"A washboiler would be better—*two* washboilersh!" suggested Toddie.

"*Now*, do you want to go home to-day, Budge?" asked Mrs. Burton, mischievously.

"I—well—I guess you'd better not remind me very much about it," replied Budge, "else maybe I'll want to. What kind of candy is it goin' to be, Aunt Alice?"

"Molasses," said Mrs. Burton.

"The stick kind or the sticky?" asked Toddie.

"Both," replied the lady.

"Oh, goody, goody!" exclaimed Toddie, clutching at his aunt's dress. "I want to kiss you."

"An' *I* want to give you an awful big hug," said Budge.

Mrs. Burton accepted these proffered tokens of esteem, to the serious disarrangement of her toilet, and afterward spent two miserable hours in trying to pacify the boys until lunch-time. The boys ate scarcely anything, and remonstrated so persistently against their aunt's appetite, that the lunch remained almost untouched. Then the lady was escorted to the kitchen by both her nephews, and there was an animated discussion as to the size of the saucepan to be used, and the boys watched the pouring of the molasses so closely that not a fly dare to assist. Then they quarreled for the right to stir the odorous mass until Mrs. Burton was obliged to allot them three-minute reliefs by the kitchen clock, and Budge declared that his turns

MAKING CANDY.

didn't last more than a second, while Toddie complained that they occupied two hours, and each boy had to assist at the critical operation of "trying," and they consumed what seemed to them long weary years in watching the paste cool itself. When, at last, Mrs. Burton pronounced one panful ready to "pull," a deep sigh of relief burst from each little chest.

"This is the way to pull candy," said Mrs. Burton, touching her fingers lightly with butter and then taking a portion of the paste from a pan and drawing it into a string in the usual manner. "And here," she said, separating the smaller portions, "is a piece for each of you."

Budge carefully oiled his fingers as he had seen his aunt do, and proceeded cautiously to draw his candy, but Toddie seized his portion with both hands, raised it to his mouth, and fastened his teeth in it. Mrs. Burton sprang at him in an instant.

"Stop, Toddie, quick! It may fasten your teeth together."

Many were the inarticulate noises, all in a tone of remonstrance, that Toddie made as his aunt forcibly removed the mass from his face. When at last he could open his mouth, he exclaimed:

"Don't *want* mine pulled—itsh too awful good the way it izh—you'll pull the good out, I'zh 'fyaid."

"You boys should have aprons on you," said Mrs. Burton. "Budge, put down your candy, run up-stairs, and tell Jane to bring down two of Toddie's aprons."

Budge hurried up-stairs, forgetting the first half of his aunt's injunction. Returning, he had just reached the foot of the main stair, when the door-bell rang. Hastily putting his candy down, he opened the door, and admitted two ladies who asked for Mrs. Burton.

"I guess she's too busy makin' candy to be bothered by any lady," said Budge, "but I'll ask her. Sit down."

Ten minutes later, Mrs. Burton, by a concentration of effort peculiar to woman, but which must ever remain a mystery to man, entered the parlor in afternoon dress, and greeted her visitors. Both rose to meet her, and with one of them rose also a rocking-chair with a cane seat; this remained in mid-air only an instant, however, for the lady's dress had not been designed for the purpose of moving furniture, and, with a sharp, ripping sound, like that of musketry file-firing afar off, her skirt soon took the appearance of a train dress, heavily puffed at the waist with fabric of another color.

Both ladies endeavored to disengage her, while Mrs. Burton turned pale and then red as she discovered the cause of the accident, while Budge's voice was heard from the doorway, saying:

"Aunt Alice, *have* you seen my candy? I laid it down

somewhere so's to let those ladies in, an' now I can't find it!"

An indignant gesture by Mrs. Burton sent Budge away pouting and grumbling, and the chambermaid was summoned, and the visitor's dress was repaired temporarily, and the accident was being laughed away, when from the kitchen there arose an appalling sound. It was compounded of shrieks, yelps, and a peculiar noise as of something being thrown upon the floor.

The noise increased; there were irregular foot-falls upon the kitchen-stairs, and at last Toddie appeared, dragging by the collar the dog Terry, from whose forefeet hung, by a slowly lengthening rope of candy, one of the pans of the unpulled paste.

"I fought if I gived him candy he would be nicer to me," explained Toddie, "so I chased him into a closet, an' put the pan up to his nose, an' told him to help hisself. An' he stuck his foot in, an'——"

Further explanation was given by deeds, not words, for as Toddie spoke, the dog kicked violently with his hind feet, disengaged himself from Toddie, and started for the door, dragging and lengthening his sweet bonds behind him upon the floor. Toddie shrieked and attempted to catch him, stepped upon the candy-rope, found himself fastened to the carpet, and burst into tears, while the visitors departed, and told stories, which by the next afternoon had developed into the statement that Mrs. Burton had been foolish enough to indulge her nephews in a candy-pulling in her parlor and upon her new carpet.

As for the boys, Budge ate some of his candy, and Toddie ate a great deal of everybody's, and had difficulty in saving a fragment for his uncle. And when he knelt in spotless white to pray that evening, he informed Heaven that *now* he understood what ladies meant when they said they had had a real sweet time.

CHAPTER XI.

"We're goin' home,
We're goin' home,
We're goin' home
To die no more"—

Sang Budge, through the hall the next morning, and he repeated the lines over and over so many times that they at last impressed themselves upon the mind of Toddie, who asked:

"Budgie, izh you tellin' the troof?"

"What 'bout?"

"Why, 'bout not dyin'; don't little boys hazh to die after goin' to live wif their uncles an' aunts for a little while?"

"Oh, of course they do; but I'm so happy I've got to sing *somethin'*; the front part of it is troof, and that's three times as big as the other part, and I can't think of any other song 'bout goin' home."

"That'sh too baddy," complained Toddie. "I fought you wazh tellin' the troof, an' I wouldn't never hazh to have a lot of dirt on my eyes so I couldn't look up into the sky."

"Why, you won't have to be bothered that way," said Budge. "When you die your spirit goes right up to heaven, an' you can look straight down froo the sky with your new eyes, an' laugh at the old dirt that thinks it's keepin' your old eyes shut up."

"Don't *want* no new eyes," said Toddie. "Eyes I've got izh good enough to see fings wif."

"But just think, Toddie," reasoned Budge, "Heaven-eyes can't get dust in 'em, or have to be washed, or be bothered with choo-choo smoke."

"Why, can't smoke get in the windows of steam-cars up in hebben?" asked Toddie.

"Why, of course not," said Budge, "not if everything's goin' to be all right up there. There ain't no choo-choos in heaven anyhow; what does angels want of choo-choos, I'd like to know, when they've got wings to fly with?"

"*I'd* never want all the choo-choos to go away, even if I had a *fousand* wingsh," said Toddie. "'Twould be such fun to fan myself wif my wings, when I was goin' froo hot old tunnels."

"Tunnels can't be hot in heaven," explained Budge, "'cause they're uncomfortable, an' nothin' can be uncomfortable in heaven. I guess there ain't any tunnels there at all—oh, yes, I guess there's little bits of ones, jus long enough to have and for little boys to ride in an' out of."

"Well, how's you goin' to ride in an' out if there ain't no choo-choos to pull the cars?"

Budge reflected and finally replied:

"Well, I tell you, Tod—I guess that's one of the things that the Bible don't tell folks about heaven. You know papa says there's lots of things the Lord don't let people know 'bout heaven, 'cause it's none of their business, an' I guess that's one of 'em."

"Wish there'd be some more Bibles, then," said Toddie, "I wantsh to know lotsh more of fingsh."

"Well, anyhow," said Budge, "we're goin' home to-day, an' that fills *me* so full I ain't got room for the littlest speck of heaven. Wonder who's goin' to take us, an' when we're a-goin', an' ev'rything? Let's go ask Uncle Harry."

"Come on!" exclaimed Toddie. "I'zh been finkin' awful hard 'bout how to get into his bedroom wifout bein' scolded, and now I know. Hurry up 'fore we forgets!"

Both boys hurried to the family chamber, and assaulted the door with fists and feet.

"'The overture of the angels,'" quoted Mr. Burton, "and 'positively their last appearance.'"

"Don't speak of it," said Mrs. Burton. "I've been crying about it in my dreams, I believe, and I'm in a condition to begin again."

"I've a great mind to make *them* cry," said the man of

the house, savagely. "No scrubbing will take marks of small shoe-toes out of painted wood."

"Let them kick to their dear little hearts' content," said Mrs. Burton. "Not a mark of that kind shall ever be insulted by a scrubbing-brush. I feel as if I'd like to go about the house and kiss everything they've touched."

"You might kiss the sounding-board of my violin, then," said Mr. Burton, "where there's an ineffaceable scratch from a nail in Toddie's shoe, placed there on the morning of your birthday anniversary. There's a nice, generous blot on the wood of the writing-desk, too, where Toddie upset a bottle of violet ink. Would that your kisses could efface the stain that the cabinet-maker says is indelible. Then there are some dingy streaks on the wall beside their bed, where they've lain crosswise, and rubbed their heads against the wall!"

"It shall remain—forever," said the lady.

"What! in your darling spare chamber?" asked Mr. Burton.

A violent mental struggle showed its indications in Mrs. Burton's face, but she replied:

"The furniture can be changed. We can put up a screen in front of the place. We'll change the room in any way excepting *their* blessed tokens of occupation."

But none of this devotion found its way through the keyhole to shame the boys into silence, for the noise increased until Mrs. Burton herself hastened to draw the bolt.

"It's us!" was the unnecessary information volunteered by Budge as the door opened, "an' we want to know when we're goin' home, an' who's goin' to take us, an' how, an' what you're goin' to give us to remember you by, an' we don't care to have it flowers, like mamma an' papa always give us, 'cause we've got plenty of them at home."

"Fruit-cake would be nicesht," suggested Toddie. "Folks 'members that an *awful* long time, 'cause when mamma once asked papa if he remembered the fruit-cake at Mrs. Birch's party he looked drefful sad, an' said he couldn't ever forget it. Say, Aunt Alish, don't you get extra nysh dinners for folks that's goin' away? Mamma alwaysh doezh; says they need it, 'cauzh folks need to be well feeded when they're goin' to travel." (The distance from the Burton residence to that of Lawrences was about a quarter of a mile.)

"You shall have a good-by dinner, Toddie dear," said Mrs. Burton, "and the very nicest one that I can prepare."

"Better make it a breaksup," suggested Toddie. "Mebbe we'll be home 'fore dinner-time."

"You sha'n't be taken until you get it, dear," replied Mrs. Burton.

"I 'spects papa'll have an awful good dinner waitin for us, too, when we get home," said Budge. "'Cause that's the way the papa in the Bible did, an' yet he had only one boy come home instead of two, an' *he'd* been bad."

"What portion of the Scriptural narrative is the child ruining now?" asked Mrs. Burton.

"Aunt Alice, don't know who you're talking about, Budge," said Mr. Burton. "Explain it to her."

"Why, that boy that his papa made a dinner out of fat veal for," said Budge, "though *I* never could see how that was a very nice dinner."

"Worse and worse!" sighed Mrs. Burton.

"Tell us all about it, old fellow," said Mr. Burton. "We don't know what you're driving at."

"Why!" exclaimed Budge, "are you bad folks that don't read your Bible-book? I thought every body knew about *him*. Why, he was a boy that went to his papa one day and told him that whatever he was goin' to give him as long as he lived, he wished he'd give it to him all at once. An' his papa did. My! wasn't he a lovely papa, though! So the boy took the money and went travelin', an' had larks. There's a picture about it all in Tommy Bryan's mamma's parlor, but I don't think it's very larky. He's just a-settin' down, with a whole lot of women actin' like geese all around him. But he had to pay money to have larks, an' he had such lots of 'em that pretty soon he didn't have no money. Say, Uncle Harry, why don't people have all the money they want?"

"That's the world's prize conundrum," said Mr. Burton. "Ask me something easier."

"I'm goin' to have all the money *I* want when I gets growed," remarked Toddie.

"How are you going to get it?" asked his uncle, with natural interest.

"Goin' to be real good an' then ask the Lord for it," said Toddie. "Wonder where the Lord keepsh the lots of nysh fings he's goin' to give good people when they ask him for 'em--money an' fings?"

"Why, in heaven, of course." said Budge.

"Hazh he got a savings bank an' a toy-store?" asked Toddie.

"Sh—h—h," instinctively whispered Mrs. Burton.

"He's only saying plainly what grown people think to themselves, my dear," said Mr. Burton. "Go on, Budge."

"Well, he didn't have any more money, an' he couldn't write to his papa for some, 'cause there wasn't any post-offices in that country, so he went to work for a man, an' the man made him feed pigs, an' he had to eat the same things as the pigs ate. I don't know whether he ate them out of a trough or not."

"It's a great pity that you are in doubt on that point," said Mr. Burton.

"He could play in the mud like the pigs, too, couldn't he?" said Toddie; "his papa was too far away to know about it, an' to say, 'Don't!' at him."

"I s'pose so," said Budge, "but I don't think a boy could feel much about playin' with mud when he had to eat with the pigs. Well, he went along bein' a pig-feeder, when all at once he 'membered that there was always enough to eat at his papa's house. Say, Uncle Harry, boys is alike everywhere ain't they?"

"I suppose so," said Mr. Burton, "present company excepted; but what reminded you of it just now?"

"Why, he wanted to go home when he couldn't hook enough from the pigs to fill his stomach, an' my papa says little boys that can't be found when their mamma wants 'em always start for home when they get hungry. That's what this boy off in another country did. Papa says the Bible don't tell whether he told the man to get another pig-feeder, or whether he just skooted in a hurry. But, anyhow, he got pretty near home, an' I guess he felt awful ashamed of himself, an' went along the back road, for in the picture in our big Bible-book his clothes are *awful* ragged an' mussy, an' he must have been sure he was goin' to get scolded, an' wish he could get in the back-door, an' go up to his room without anybody seein' him."

"Oh, Harry!" exclaimed Mrs. Burton. "This is growing perfectly dreadful—it's positively sacrilegious."

"The application is the only sacred part of the original, my dear," said Mr. Burton, "and you may trust that boy to discover the point of anything I wish doctors of divinity were half as quick to do so. Go ahead, Budge."

"Well," said Budge, "he was sneakin' along, an' gettin' behind trees an' fences whenever he saw anybody comin' that he knew, when all at once his papa saw him. Papas always *can* see further than anybody else, I believe, an' they always kind o' know when their boys are comin', an' they look just as if they'd always been standin' right there waitin' for 'em. An' that pig-feeder's papa ran right out the house without his hat on—that's the way he is in the picture in the Bible-book—an' grabbed him, an' kissed him, an' hugged him so hard that he had to grunt, an'——"

"An' he didn't say, 'Why, how *did* you get your clozhesh so dirty?' eiver," said Toddie.

"No, indeed," said Budge. "An' the pig-feeder said he'd been a bad boy, an' he guessed he'd better eat his dinner in the kitchen after that, but his papa wouldn't let him. He put clean clothes on him, an' gave him a new pair of shoes, an' put a ring on his finger."

"Ringsh ain't good to eat," remarked Toddie. "I fwallowed one once, *I* did, an' it didn't taste nohow at all. An' then I had to take some nashty medshin', an the ring came *un*-fwallowed again."

"He didn't give him the ring to eat, you silly boy," said Budge. "Rings squeeze fingers all the time, an' let folks know how the folks that give 'em the rings want to squeeze *them* all the time. Then they killed a whole calf—'cause the pig-feeder was *awful* empty, you know—an' they had a jolly old time. An' the pig-feeder's big brother heard 'em all cuttin' up, an' he was real cross about it, 'cause he'd always been good, and there hadn't ever been any tea-parties made for *him*. But his papa said, 'Oh, don't say a word; we've got your brother back again—just think of *that*, my boy.' I'm awful sorry for that big brother, though; *I* know how he felt, for when Tod's bad an' I'm good, papa just takes Tod in his lap an' talks to him, an' hugs him, an' I feels awful lonesome an' wish I wasn't good a bit."

"And what do you suppose the bad boy's mamma did when she saw him?" asked Mrs. Burton.

"Oh," said Budge, "I guess she didn't say anything, but just looked so sad at him that he made up his mind he wouldn't ever do a naughty thing again as long as he lived, an' after that he'd stand behind her chair whole half-hours at a time, just to look at her when she wouldn't catch him at it."

"And what do you think that whole story means, Budge?" asked Mrs. Burton, determined to impress at least one prominent theological deduction upon her nephew

"Why, it means that good papas can always see when bad boys is real ashamed of themselves," said Budge, "an' know it's best to be real sweet to 'em then, an' that papas that *can't* see, and don't know better than to scold 'em then, needn't ever expect to see their bad little boys come home again."

Mrs. Burton started, and her husband laughed inwardly at this application; but the lady recovered herself, and returned in haste to her point.

"Don't you think it's intended to teach us anything about the Lord?" she asked.

"Why, yes," said Budge. "Of course, if He's the best of all papas, He'll be better to his bad children than any other good papas know how to be!"

"That's what the story is meant to teach," said Mrs. Burton.

"Why, I thought everybody knew *that* about the Lord," said Budge.

"If they did, Jesus would never have told the story," said Mrs. Burton.

"Oh, I s'pose those old Jews had to be told it," said Budge, "'cause folks used to be awful bad to their children, an' believed the Lord would be awful cruel to *them*."

"People need to be told the same story now, Budge," continued Mrs. Burton. "They love to hear it, and know how good the Lord is willing to be to them!"

"Do they love it better than to learn how good they ought to be to *their* children?" asked Budge. "Then I think they're piggish. I wouldn't like my papa an' mamma to be that way. They say that it's gooder to care for what you can give than what you can get. An' Uncle Harry hasn't told us yet when we are goin' home, an' who is goin' to take us."

"Your papa is going to come for you as he returns from the city," said Mr. Burton. "I think he wants to tell you some things before you go home. You little boys don't know yet how to act in a house where there are sick mammas and little babies!"

"Oh, yes, we do!" said Budge. "All we've got to do is to sit still, and look at 'em with all our mights!"

"Only dzust dzump up ev'ry two or free minutes to kiss 'em," suggested Toddie.

"Yes," said Budge, "and to pat their cheeks."

"An' to put nice things to eat in their mouths, like papa an' mamma does to *us* when we're sick," added Budge.

"An' make music for 'em," said Toddie.

"An' give 'em pennies," said Budge.

"An shake their savin's banks for 'em to make the pennies rattle, like Budge did for me once when I was too sick to rattle my own bank," said Toddie, bestowing a frantic hug upon his brother.

"An' put the room to rights for 'em," said Budge.

"An' bring 'em in nice mud pies all ready baked, like I did once for Budgie, to play wif on the bed when he was sick," said Toddie.

"An' dance for 'em," suggested Budge. "That's the way I used to do for Baby Phillie, an' it always made him so happy."

"An' put up pictures on the wall for 'em," said Toddie. "We's got whole newspapers full that we's cutted out up in your garret, and there's a whole bottle of mucilage——"

"My war-file of *Frank Leslie's Illustrated Newspaper!*" exclaimed Mr. Burton. "How did they find that? Oh, this cross of love!"

"Whole bottle of mucilage in papa's room to stick 'em on wif," continued Toddie, "an' mamma's room is nice pink, like the leaves of my scrap-book that pictures look so pretty on."

"And these are the child-ideas of being good and useful!" exclaimed Mrs. Burton, as the boys forgot everything else in the discovery of their uncle's razor-strop with an extension arrangement at the end.

"Yes," sighed Mr. Burton, "and they're not much nearer the proper thing, in spite of their good intentions, than the plans of grown people for the management of children, the reformation of the world, and a great many other things."

"Harry!" exclaimed Mrs. Burton, in injured tones.

"No personal allusion, my dear," said Mr. Burton, quickly. "I'd no thought of anything of the kind. Both adults and children mean well enough; the difference is, that the former wonder why their ideas are not appreciated, while with the children the energies of parents and teachers are devoted to treating imperfect ideas as great sins. How many children could do the kindnesses which Budge and Toddie have devised in the tenderness of their dear little hearts, and not be scolded and whipped for their pains? What hosts of children I know who have had all the good blood and kind heart and honest head scolded and beaten out of them, and only the baser qualities of their natures allowed to grow, and these only because in youth many of them are dormant and don't make trouble!"

"Why, Harry! What a preacher you are—what a *terrible* preacher!" exclaimed Mrs. Burton.

"Where does the terror come in?" asked Mr. Burton, with signs of that indignation which every man with an idea in advance of his generation must frequently experience.

"Why, to imply that there's so much injustice being done to children," said the lady.

"Of course the saying of it is worse than the fact of its existence," remarked Mr. Burton, with a curl of lip.

"Please don't speak in that cruel way," said Mrs. Burton. "It isn't anything of the sort—excepting for a moment or two."

Mr. Burton apologized and restored confidence without saying a word, and then the couple turned instinctively to look at the first causes of their conversation, but the boys were gone.

"The tocsin of their souls, the dinner-bell—breakfast-bell, I mean—has probably sounded," said Mr. Burton, "and I'm as hungry as a bear myself. Let's descend, and see what they've succeeded in doing within five brief minutes."

The Burtons found the dining-room, but not the boys, and the chambermaid was sent in search of them. The meal was slowly consumed, but the boys did not appear.

"You'd better have the cook prepare something additional," suggested Mr. Burton, as he arose and started for his train. "The appetite of the small boy is a principal that accumulates frightful usury in a very small while after maturity."

Mrs. Burton acted upon her husband's suggestion, and busied herself about household affairs for an hour or more, until, learning that the boys had not yet arrived, she strolled out in some apprehension to search for them.

Supposing that they might have been overpowered by their impatience so far as to have gone home at once, she visited the residence of her sister-in-law, and inquired of the faithful Mike.

"Dhivil a bit have they been here," replied Michael. "Ain't we eye-sore for the soight of 'em all the whoile? They're nowhere about here, rest ye aisy."

"I'm afraid they may be lost!" exclaimed Mrs Burton.

Mike burst into a prolonged horse-laugh, and then, recovering himself by sundry contortions and swallowings, he replied:

"Beggin' yer pardon, ma'am, but I couldn't help it—as the Blessed Virgin is smoilin' in heaven I cuddent—but thim byes can niver be lost. *Lost*, is it? Cud ye lose a ghost or a bird? They'll foind their way anywhere they've been once, an' if they haven't been there before, they'll belave they have, an' foind their way out all right. Save yer boddher till dinner-toime, an', mark me wurruds. ye'll foind yev no nade av it. Lost!"

And Mike burst into another laugh that he hurried into the stable to hide, while Mrs. Burton returned to her own home with a mind almost quiet.

The morning ended in lunch-time, however, and no small boys appeared at the table. Mrs. Burton's fears came back with increased strength, and she hurried off again to Mike, and implored him to go in search of the children.

The sight of an ugly-looking tramp or two by the way

suggested the mystery of Charley Ross to Mrs. Burton, and brought some miserable tears to her eyes. Even the doubting Mike, when he learned that the children had eaten nothing that day, grew visibly alarmed, and mounted one of his master's horses in hot haste.

"Where are you going first, Mike?" asked Mrs. Burton.

"Dhivil a bit do I know," exclaimed Mike; "but I'm goin' to foind 'em, an' may the blessed saints go wid me!"

Away galloped Mike, and Mrs. Burton, fearing lest the alarm might reach the boys' mother, hurried home, started the cook upon one road, the chambermaid on another, and herself took a third, while Mike sought the candy-store, the school-house, sundry bridges over brooks, and various other places that boys delight in.

Mrs. Burton's own course was along a road leading up a rugged, heavily-wooded hill, called by courtesy a mountain, but she paused so many times to call, to listen, to step considerably out of her way to see if dimly descried figures were not those of her nephews, and to discover that what seemed in the forest to be boyish figures were only stumps of bushes, that she spent at least two hours upon the road, which doubled so many times upon itself Suddenly she saw, on the rugged road beyond her, a familiar figure dragging a large green bough.

"Budge!" she screamed, and ran toward him. The

little figure turned its head, and Mrs. Burton was shocked to see a very haggard face, whose whiteness intensified the staring eyes, pink, distended nostrils, and thin, drawn lips of her nephew. And upon the bough, holding to one of the upper sprigs tightly with one hand, while with the other he clutched something green and crumpled, lay Toddie, dust-incrusted from head to foot.

"Oh, what has happened!" exclaimed Mrs. Burton.

Toddie raised his head and explained:

"I'zhe a shotted soldier bein' tookted to where the shooters can't catch me, like sometimes they used to be in the war."

As for Budge, he dropped in the road and cried.

"Oh, what *is* it?" cried Mrs. Burton, kneeling beside Toddie and taking him in her arms, and Toddie replied:

"*Ow!*"

"Budge, dear," exclaimed Mrs. Burton, replacing Toddie and hurrying to his brother, "what *has* happened? *Do* tell me!"

Budge opened his eyes and mouth very reluctantly and replied in a very thin voice:

"Wait till I get alive again, an' I'll tell you. I havn't got many words inside of me now—they're all dropped out, I'se so tired, an' oh——"

Budge closed his eyes again. Mrs. Burton picked him up tenderly, sat upon a large stone, rocked back and forth with him, kissed him repeatedly, and cried over him, while Toddie turned upon his stomach, surveyed the scene with apparent satisfaction, and remarked :

"Say, Aunt Alish, its djolly to be a shotted soldier."

Budge slowly recovered, put his arms around his aunt very tightly, and finally said :

"Oh, Aunt Alice, 'twas *awful!*"

"Tell me all about it, dear," said Mrs. Burton, "when you feel well enough. Where have you been all day? aunty's heart has been almost broken about you."

"Why, you see," said Budge, "we wanted to do something nice for *you*, 'fore we went home to stay, 'cause you've been so nice to us. Why, when we talked about it we couldn't think of a single unpleasant thing you'd done to us, though I'm sure you *have* done some. Any how, we couldn't 'member any."

"'Cept sayin' 'Don't!' lotsh of timesh," remarked Toddie.

"Well," said Budge, "Tod thought 'bout *that*, but we made up our minds perhaps we needed that said to us. An' we couldn't think of anything nicer than to get you some wild flowers, *ev'ry* body's got *tame* flowers, you know, so we thought wild ones would be nicer. An' we thought we could get 'em 'fore breakfas' if we'd hurry up; so off we came right up to the foot of the mountain, but there wasn't any—I guess they wasn't awake yet, or else they'd gone to sleep. Then we didn't know *what* to do."

"'Cept get you some bych (birch) bark," said Toddie.

"Yes," said Budge, "but birch bark is to eat an' not to look at, an' we wanted to give you somethin' you could see, an' remember us a few days by."

"An' all of a sudden *I* said 'fynes!'" (ferns) said Toddie.

"Yes," said Budge, "Tod *said* it first, but I *thought* it the same second, an' there's such *lovely* ferns up in the rocks—don't you see?"

Mrs. Burton looked and shuddered; the cliff above her head was a hundred feet high, jagged all over its front, yet from each crevice exquisite ferns posed their graceful fronds before the cold gray of the rock.

"'Twasn't here," said Budge: "'twas way up around the corner where the rocks ain't so high, but they're harder to climb. We climbed up here first."

"Oh, you dreadful, darling children!" exclaimed Mrs. Burton, giving Budge a squeeze of extra severity. "To think of two little children going up such a dreadful place! Why, it makes me dizzy to see your Uncle Harry do it."

"Ain't childrens when we climbs mountainsh," asserted Toddie. "We'zh *mans* then."

"Well," continued Budge, "we got lots, and throwed

each one away 'cause we kept seein' nicer ones higher up. Say, Aunt Alice, what's the reason things higher up, always look extra nice?"

"I know," said Toddie.

"Why is it, then, Toddie?" asked Mrs. Burton.

"'Cauzh theyzh closer to hebben," said Toddie. "G'won, Budgie—*I* likes to hear about it, too."

"Well," said Budge, "at last we got to a place where the rocks all stopped an' some more began, an' upon them was the loveliest ferns of all."

"An' I went up that mountain fyst, *I* did," said Toddie.

"Yes, Tod *did*, the blessed little sassy rascal," said Budge, blowing a kiss to his brother. "I told him I didn't believe that any ferns was nicer than any others, but he said. "Lord 'll make some, so then for Aunt Alish.' And up he went, just like a spider."

"Went up *fyst*," said Toddie.

"Course you did," said Budge, "'cause I didn't go up at all. And Tod was pullin' at a big fern with his back to me, an' the first thing I knew there he was in air layin' down sideways on nothin'. Then he hollered."

"'Cauzh I comed down bunk on whole lotsh of little wocks," explained Toddie. "But I didn't lose the fyne—here 'tizh!" And Toddie held up a badly crushed and wilted ball of something that had once been a fern, seeing which Mrs. Burton sat Budge upon the stone, hurried tc Toddie, thrust the bruised fern into her bosom, and kissed its captor soundly.

"Hold me some more," said Budge. "I don't feel very good yet."

"Then what did you do?" asked Mrs. Burton, resuming her position as nurse.

"Why, Tod went on hollerin', an' he couldn't walk, so I helped him down to the road, an' he couldn't walk yet——"

Mrs. Burton hastened again to Toddie and carefully examined his legs without finding any broken bones.

"The hurt is in the bottom part of my leg an' the top part of my foot," said Toddie, who had sprained his ankle.

"An' he just hollered 'mam-*ma*' an' 'pa-*pa*' so sad," continued Budge "An' 'twas awful. An' I looked up the road, an' there wasn't anybody, an' down the road, an' there wasn't anybody, an' down the front of the mountain, an' there wasn't anybody, an' I didn't know what to do, 'cause it wouldn't do to go way off home to tell, when a poor little brother was feelin' so dreadful bad. Then I remembered how papa said he'd some time seen shot soldiers carried away when there wasn't any wagons. So I pulled at the limb of a tree to get the thing to drag him on.

"Why, Budge!" exclaimed Mrs. Burton. "You don't

mean to say you got that bough all alone by yourself, do you?"

"Well, no—I guess not," said Budge, hesitatingly. "I pull at one after another, but not one of them would split, and then I thought of somethin', and kneeled right down by the tree, an' told the Lord all about it, an' told Him I knew He didn't want poor little hurt Tod to lie their all day, an' wouldn't He *please* help me break a limb to draw him on. An' when I got up off my knees I was as strong as forty thousand horses. I don't think I needed the Lord to help me a bit then. An' I just gave one pull at the limb, and down it came kersplit, an' I put Tod on it, and dragged him. But I tell you it was hard!"

"'Twash fun, too," said Toddie, "'cept when it went where there was little rocks in the road, an' they came up an' hitted the hurt playshe."

"I dragged it in the soft parts of the road," said Budge, "whenever I could, but sometimes there wasn't any soft place all across the road. An things jumped inside of me—that little heart-engine, you know—*awful.* I could only go about a dozen steps without stoppin' to rest, an' then Tod stopped cryin' an' said he was hungry, an' that reminded me that I was hungry, too."

"But we didn't lose the fyne," said Toddie.

Mrs. Burton took the memento from her breast and kissed it.

"Why," said Budge, "you *do* like it awful, don't you? All right, then, Tod an' me don't care for brothers an' hurts then, do we, Tod?"

"No, indeedy," said Toddie. "Not when we can ride like shotted soldiers, an' get home to get breksup an' lunch togevver."

"Neither of you shall have any more trouble about getting home," said Mrs. Burton. "Just sit here quietly while I go and send a carriage for you!"

"My!" said Budge. "That'll be lovely—won't it, Tod? Ain't you glad you got hurt? But say, Aunt Alice, haven't you got any crackers in your pockets?"

"Why, no—certainly not," exclaimed the lady, temporarily losing her tenderness.

"Oh," said Budge, "I thought you might have. Papa always does when he goes out to look for us when we stay away from home a good while."

Suddenly a horse's hoofs were heard on the road below.

"I shouldn't wonder if that was Mike," said Mrs. Burton. "He has been out on horseback looking for you!"

"*I* shouldn't wonder if 'twas papa," said Budge. "He's the funniest man for always comin' anywhere just when we need him most."

"An' wif crackers," remarked Toddie.

The clattering hoofs came nearer, though slower, and

finally, true to the children's intuitions, around the bend of the road came Tom Lawrence on horseback, an old army haversack and canteen slung over his shoulder.

"Pa-*pa!*" shouted both boys; "hooray!" Tom Lawrence waved his hat, and Toddie shrieked, "He's got the crackers—I see the bag!"

The father reined up suddenly and dismounted.

Budge rushed to his arms, and Toddie exclaimed:

"Papa, guesh it's along time since you's seen a shotted soldier, ain't it?"

Then Toddie was placed in the saddle, and Budge behind him, and the precious haversack was opened and found to contain sandwiches, and both boys tried to drink out of the canteen and poured a great deal of water in their bosoms, and Tom led the horse carefully, and Mrs. Burton walked upon one side, with a hand under Toddie's lame leg to keep the bruised ankle from touching the saddle, and she did not swerve from the middle of the dusty road, even when carriages full of stylish acquaintances were met, and both little heroes, like men of larger growth, forgot at once that they had ever been heroic, and they prattled as inconsequently as any couple of silly children could have done, and the horse was led by a roundabout road so that no one might see the party and apprise Mrs. Lawrence that anything unusual had happened, and the boys were heavily bribed to tell their mother nothing until their father had first explained, and they were carried in, each in his father's arms to kiss their mamma, and when they undressed and went to bed, the sister-baby, was by special dispensation of the nurse, allowed to lie between them for a few moments, and the evening ceremonies were prolonged indefinitely by the combined acts of boys and parent, and then Budge knelt and prayed.

"Dear Lord, wer'e awful glad to get back home again, 'cause nobody can be like papa and mamma to us, an' I'm so thankful I don't know what to do for bein' made so strong when I wanted to break that limb off of the tree, an' bless dear Aunt Alice for findin' us, and bless poor Mike *more*, 'cause he tried to find us an' was disappointed, an' make every little boy's papa just like ours, to come to 'em just where they need him, just like—You. Amen."

And Toddie shut his eyes in bed, and said: "Dee Lord, I went up the mountain fyst—don't forget *that*. Amen."

CHAPTER XII.

THERE was a little family conclave at the Lawrence home a fortnight later. No deliberative meeting had been intended; quite the contrary, for Mrs. Lawrence was on that day to make her first appearance at the dinner-table within a month, and Mrs. Burton and her husband were invited to drop in informally on the occasion, and they had been glad enough to do so, although the boys, who had been allowed to dine that night with the family in honor of the occasion, conversed so volubly that no other person at the table could speak without interruption. But there came an hour when the boys could no longer prolong the usual preliminaries of going to bed, although they kissed their parents and visitors once, as a matter of course; a second time, to be sure that they had done it; and a third time, to assure themselves that they had forgotten nobody. Then several chats were interrupted by various juvenile demands, pleas and questions from the upper floor; but as, when Tom Lawrence went in person to answer the last one, he found both boys sleeping soundly, the family devoted themselves to each other with the cordiality of close friends who had long been separated. They talked of what was going on in the world, and a great deal that might be going on but was not, the blame being due to persons who did not think as they did; they sang, played, quoted books, talked pictures and bric-à-brac, and then Mrs. Lawrence changed the entire course of the conversation by promising to replace Mrs. Burton's chair, which the dog Terry had destroyed by special arrangement of the boys.

"You shan't do anything of the sort," said Mrs. Burton. "Just keep the dear little scamps from playing such pranks on any one who don't happen to love them so well, and I'll forgive them."

"You don't imagine for a moment that they knew what the result would be when they tied Terry to the chair, do you?" asked Mrs. Lawrence.

"Never!" exclaimed Mrs. Burton emphatically. "But they *did* it, and it might have happened somewhere else, with some one who didn't love them so well, and what would they have thought?"

"She means that strangers would have imagined your boys to be a couple of little boors, Nell," said Mr. Burton, to his sister.

"Strangers know nothing whatever about other people's children," said Mrs. Lawrence, with considerable dignity "and they should therefore have nothing to do with them, and pass no opinions upon them. No one estimates children by what they are; they judge only by the amount of trouble they make. Some bloodless little manikins—they're almost idiots, poor little things!—go through childhood as pinks of propriety, simply because they never do anything out of the way What do people think about the good things and loving things that the helpless, almost soulless, little things should do, but don't!"

"Now you've done it, Mistress Alice!" said Mr. Burton to his wife. "It is better to meet a she-bear that is robbed of her whelps, than a mother whose children are criticised by any one but herself."

"*I've* done it?" exclaimed Mrs. Burton. "Who translated my quiet remark into something offensive enough to make *any* lady angry? Besides, you've misapplied Scripture only to suggest things worse yet. If I'm not mistaken, the proverb about the she-bear and her whelps has something in it about a fool and his folly. Do you mean to insinuate such insulting ideas about your sister and her darlings?"

But no amount of badinage could make Mrs. Lawrence forget that some implied advice was secreted in her sister-in-law's carefully-worded remark, so she continued:

"I'm extremely sorry they had to go to you, but I couldn't imagine what better to do. I wish Tom could have staid at home all the while to take care of them. I hope, if we ever die, they may follow us at once—nothing is so dreadful as the idea of one's children being perpetually misunderstood by some one else, and having their dear, honest little hearts hardened and warped just when they should be cared for most patiently and tenderly."

"Why, Helen!" exclaimed Mrs. Burton, changing her seat so as to take Mrs. Lawrence's hand, "I'd *die* for your children at any time, if it would do them any good."

"I know it, you dear girl," said Mrs. Lawrence, recovering her natural manner, and not entirely unashamed of her outburst of feelings; "but you do not understand it all—as you will, some day. The children trouble me worse than they ever did, or can, any one else; but it *isn't* their fault, and I know it, and can endure it. No one else can—I am sure I don't know how to blame people who are annoyed by pranks naturally annoying."

"Then what's to be done with youngsters in general?" asked Mrs. Burton.

"They're to be kept at home," said Mrs. Lawrence—'kept under the eye of father or mother continually, until they are large enough to trust, and the age at which they're to be trusted should not be determined by the impatience of their parents or those appointed to take charge of them."

"Don't be frightened, Allie," said Tom. "Helen had

some of these notions before she had any boys of her own to defend—they're of general application."

"They're certainly not the result of my children's happy experiences with the best aunt and uncle that ever lived," said Mrs. Lawrence, caressing her adopted sister's hand. "If you could hear the boys' praises of you both, you'd grow insufferably vain, and imagine yourselves born to manage orphan asylums."

"Heaven forbid!" exclaimed Mrs. Burton, the immediate result of her utterance being the partial withdrawal of Mrs. Lawrence's hand. "There are only two children in the family——"

"Three," corrected Mrs. Lawrence, promptly.

"Oh, bless me, what *have* I said!" exclaimed Mrs. Burton. "Well, there are only three children in the family, and they are not enough to found an asylum, while I feel utterly unfitted to care for any child that I don't know very well and love very dearly."

"Is it possible that any one can learn so much in so short a time?" exclaimed Tom Lawrence. "Harry, my boy, you're to be congratulated."

"Upon educating me?" asked Mrs. Burton, with an assumed pout.

"Upon the rare wisdom with which he selected a wife —or the special favor he found at the court where matches are made," explained Tom.

"Harry didn't select me at all," said Mrs. Burton. "Budge did it for him, so of course the match was decreed in heaven. But may I know of what my sudden acquisition of knowledge consists? If there is anything in my experience with the boys that I am not to feel humiliated about, I should be extremely glad to know of it. I went into the Valley of Humiliation within an hour of their arrival, and since then I've scarcely been out of it."

"If it weren't for being suspected of a tendency to throw moral deductions at people," said Tom, "I would say that that same Valley of Humiliation is very prolific in discoveries. But—preaching aside—you have made a rare discovery in learning that no one can manage children without first loving them; even a heart full of love generally has to make room for a good deal of sorrow over blunders and failures."

"To say nothing of the way that some affection thins the hair on the top of a father's head," suggested Mr. Burton.

"Personalities of that sort are out of order until I reach three-score years," said Tom.

"I've learned that affection is absolutely necessary," said Mrs. Burton; "but I confess that I don't see clearly that love requires that one should be trampled upon, wheedled, made of no account, and without authority in one's own house; submit to everything, in fact——"

"Now you've done it again!" whispered Mr. Burton to his wife, as Helen Lawrence's cheeks began again to flush, and that maternal divinity replied:

"Does the Parent of all of us resign His authority when he humors us in *our* childish ways, because we can't comprehend any greater ones? Every concession is followed by growth on the part of His children, if they are honest; when they're not, it seems to me the concessions aren't made. But *my* children *are* honest."

Mrs. Burton's lips were parting, seeing which her husband whispered:

"Don't!"

There was a moment or two of silence, and then Mrs. Burton asked:

"How are people to know when they're being imposed upon by children? You can't apply to the funny little beings the rules that explain the ways of grown people."

"Is it the most dreadful thing in the world to be imposed upon by a child?" asked Tom. "We never impose upon *them*, do we? We never give them unfair answers, arbitrary commands, unkind restrictions, simply to save ourselves a little extra labor or thought?"

"Now, Tom!" exclaimed Mrs. Burton. "I didn't do anything of the sort, I'm sure."

"Why will you display so touchy a conscience, then?"

whispered her husband. "If you continue to put up your defenses the instant Tom launches a criticism, he'll begin to suspect you of dreadful cruelty to the boys."

"Not I," laughed Tom.

"She had *you* to reform for half a year before the boys visited her," said Helen, "and you still live."

"But, Tom—seriously now—you don't mean to have me infer that you think children shouldn't be made to mind, and be prevented from doing things that can bother their elders?" asked Mrs. Burton.

"Certainly they should learn to obey," said Tom; "but I'd rather they wouldn't, if at the same time they must learn—as in general they can't help doing—that obedience is imposed more for the benefit of their elders than themselves."

"*I* was always taught to mind" said Mrs. Burton, with the not unusual, though always unconscious, peculiarity of supposing the recital of her own personal experience to be an unanswerable argument and precedent.

"Do you find the habit still strong in her, Harry?" asked Tom.

"Do I?" exclaimed Harry, with a mock-tragic air. "'Could I the horrors of my prison-house unfold,' you would see that the obedient member of the Burton family never appears in dresses."

"Certainly not," said Mrs. Burton. "Didn't he promise to be mine to command, and shall I neglect my responsibilities? I obeyed my parents."

"And never doubted that their orders were wise, necessary and beneficent, of course?" asked Lawrence.

"Tom! Tom!" said Helen, warningly, "if you don't want Alice to abuse other people's children, be careful what you say about other children's parents. Don't play grand inquisitor."

"Oh! not at all!" said Tom, hastily. "Only I should like to borrow woman's curiosity for awhile, and have it gratified in this particular case."

"I don't know that I always admitted the wisdom of my parents' commands," said Mrs. Burton. "But how could I? I was only a child."

"You rendered unquestioning obedience—in spirit as well as in act—when you became a young lady, then?" pursued Tom.

"No, I didn't—there!" exclaimed Mrs. Burton: "but what return can a child make for parental care and suffering, except to at least seem to be a model of compliance with its parents' desires!"

"Good!" exclaimed Harry. "And what can a husband—who knows his own way is best—do to recompense wifely companionship, but to meekly do as his wife wants him to do—no matter how incorrect her ideas——"

"He can listen to reason, and not be a conceited

goose!" said Mrs. Burton; "and he can refrain from impeding the flow of brotherly instruction."

"Oh! thank you—thank you!" said Tom. "I hope your irony may sharpen my wits a little, for you've set me upon my hobby between you, and I must ride it until I'm tired out."

"Don't be priggish, Tom!" said Helen, warningly.

"I'll try not," said Tom; "but one can't tell unwelcome truths in this world without being a prig—by reputation, at least."

"Tom shall say what he pleases," said Mrs. Burton. "I command it."

Mrs. Lawrence's smile showed that she would be satisfied with the result, and her husband continued:

"Children—ninety-nine one-hundredths of those I've seen, at least—are treated as necessary nuisances by their parents. The good fathers and mothers would be horrified to realize this truth. And when it accidentally presents itself—as it frequently does to any one with heart and head—its appearance is so unpleasing and perplexing that they promptly take refuge in tradition. Weren't they brought up in the same way? To be sure, it's the application of the same rule that has always made the ex-slave the cruelest of overseers and the ex-servant the worst of masters; but such comparisons are odious to one's pride and what chance has self-respect when pride steps down before it?"

"Poor human nature!" sighed Harry. "You'll get to Adam's fall pretty soon, won't you, Tom?"

"Don't fear!" laughed Mr. Lawrence. "It's the falling of other people that troubles me—that and their willingness to stay down when they've tumbled, and the calmness with which they can lie quiet and crush poor little children, who aren't responsible for being under them. Adam knew enough to wish himself back in his honorable position; but most parents have had no lofty position to which they can look longingly back, and there are but few of them that can remember any such place having been in the possession of any member of their respective families."

"But what is to be done, even if any one wants to live up to your ideal standard as a guardian of children?" asked Mrs. Burton. "Submit to any and every imposition, allow every misdeed to go unpunished. be the ruled instead of the ruler?"

"Oh, no," said Tom; "it's something a great deal harder than that. It's to live for the children instead of one's self."

"And have all your nice times spoiled and your plans upset?"

"Yes, unless they're really of more value than human life and human character," replied Tom. "You indicated the proper starting-point in your last remark; if you'll study that for yourself you'll learn a great deal more than I can tell you, and learn it more pleasantly, too."

"I don't *want* to study," said Mrs. Burton, "when I can get my information at second hand."

"Go on, Tom," said Mr. Burton; "continue to appear in your character of the 'Parental Encyclopedist.' We'll try to stop one ear, so that what goes in at the other shan't be lost."

"I only want to say that the plans and good times which Alice alludes to as being spoiled by the children, are what ruin every promising generation. The child should be taught; but, instead of that, he is only restrained; he should be encouraged to learn the meaning and essence of whatever of the inevitable is forced upon him from year to year, but he soon learns that children's questions are as unwelcome as tax-collectors or lightning-rod men. And it's astonishing how few hints are necessary to give a child the habit of retiring into himself, and from there to such company as he can find to tolerate him."

"You needn't fear for *your* boys, Tom," said Mr. Burton. "I'd pay handsomely for the discovery of a single question which they had ever wanted to ask, but refrained from putting"

"And what myriads of them they can ask—not that there's anything wrong about it, the little darlings!" said Mrs. Burton.

"I am glad of it," said Tom, "but I hope they'll never again have to go to any one but their mother and me for information."

"Now, Tom, there you go again," said Mrs. Burton. "I don't believe I ever refused them an answer, or answered unkindly."

"Certainly you haven't," said Tom. "Excuse a stale quotation—'the exception proves the rule'—and I've really been nervously anxious about the soundness of *this* rule, until you were brought into the family, for I never knew another exception."

"May I humbly suggest that a certain brother-in-law existed before the boys had an Aunt Alice?" asked Mr. Burton.

"Oh, yes," said Tom, "but he was too well rewarded for the little he did to be worthy of consideration."

Mrs. Burton inclined her head in acknowledgment of her brother-in-law's compliment, and asked:

"But do you think all children's questions are put with any distinct attention? Don't you imagine that they ask a great many because they don't know what else to do, or because they want to put off obedience to some order or other, or because they want to—to—"

"To talk against time, she means, Tom," said Mr. Burton.

"Very likely," said Tom; "but the answers are what

are of consequence, no matter what the motive of the questions may be."

"What an idea!" exclaimed Mrs. Burton. "Really, Tom, aren't you afraid you are losing yourself?"

"I hadn't noticed it," said Tom. "But perhaps I may be able to explain myself more clearly. You go to church?"

"Regularly—every Sunday," responded Mrs. Burton promptly.

"And always with the most reverent feelings, of course. You never find your mind full of idle questionings, or mere curious wonderings, or even a perfect blank, or a circle upon which your thoughts chase themselves around to their starting-place without aim or motive?"

"How well you know the ways of humdrum mind, Tom!" said Mrs. Burton. "You didn't learn them from personal experience, of course?"

"I wish I hadn't," said Tom. "But supposing you've, at some few times in your life, gone into the sanctuary in such frames of mind, did you never have them changed by what you heard, and did you never have the very common experience of learning that it is at these very moments of weakness, indecision, blankness, childishness, or whatever you may please to call it, the mind becomes peculiarly retentive of whatever of real value that happens to strike it?"

Mrs. Burton reflected, and by silence signified her assent; but she was not fully satisfied with the explanation, for she asked:

"Do you think, then, that all the ways of children are just as they should be—that they never ask questions from any but heaven-ordained motives—that they are utterly devoid of petty guile?"

"They're human, I believe," said Mr. Lawrence, "and full of human weaknesses; but any other human beings—present company excepted, of course—should know by experience how little malice there is in the most annoying people. Certainly children *do* copy the faults of their elders, and—oh, woe is me!—inherit the failings of their ancestors; but it is astonishing how few they seem to have when the observer will forget himself and honestly devote himself to their good. I confess it *does* need the wisdom of Solomon to discover when they are honest, and when they are inclined to be tricky."

"And can you inform us where the wisdom of Solomon is to be procured for the purpose?" asked Mrs. Burton.

"From the source at which Solomon obtained it, I suppose," said Tom Lawrence; "from an honest, unselfish mind, and the assisting Power which is quick to search out and help the honest mind wherever it is. But it is so much easier to trust to selfishness and its twin-demon, suspicion, that nothing but a pitying Providence saves children from reform-schools and penitentiaries."

"But the superiority of adults—their right to demand implicit, unquestioning obedience——"

"Is the most vicious, debasing tyranny that the world was ever cursed by!" interrupted Tom Lawrence with startling emphasis. "It gave to the old Romans power of life and death over their children; it cast some of the vilest blots upon the pages of Holy Writ. Nowadays it is worse, for then it worked its principal mischief upon the body, but now 'I say unto you fear not them that kill the body, but'—excuse a free rendering—'fear them who cast both soul and body into hell!' You're orthodox, I believe."

Mrs. Burton shuddered, but her belief in the rights of the adult, in which she had inherited from a line of ancestors reaching back to Adam, or to Protoplasm, if the scientists prefer to extend the dismal line of evil-doers, was more powerful than her horror, and the latter was quickly overcome by the former.

"Then adults have no rights that children are bound to respect?" she asked.

"Yes; the right of undoing the failures of their own education, and doing it for the benefit of beings for whose existence they are wholly responsible. Can you imagine a greater crime than calling a soul into existence without its own desire and volition, and then making it your slave instead of making yourself its friend?"

"Why, Tom, you're perfectly dreadful!" exclaimed Mrs. Burton. "One would suppose that parents were a lot of pre-ordained monsters!"

"They're worse," said Tom, "they're unthinking people with a great deal of self-satisfaction and a reputation for correctness of life. Malicious people are easily caught and kept out of mischief by the law; the respectable, unintentional evil-doers are those who make most of the trouble and suffering in the world."

"And you propose to go through life, dying deaths daily, for the sake of those children," said Alice, "rather than make them what you would like them to be?"

"No," said Tom. "I propose to live a new life daily, and learn what life should be, for the sake of making them what I would like them to be, for I don't value them so much as conveniences and playthings as for what they may be to themselves and the world that so sorely needs good men."

"And women," added Mrs. Lawrence. "I do believe you've forgotten the baby, you heartless wretch!"

"I accept the amendment," said Tom, "but I didn't make it myself, for the world has already more good women than it begins to appreciate."

"Bless me! what a quantity of governing that poor

sister-baby will get, then!" said Mrs. Burton "But of course *you* don't call it governing—you'll denominate it self-immolation; you'll lose your remaining hair and grow ten years older in the first year of the little darling's life."

"I shouldn't wonder," said Tom, with an expression of countenance which banished the smiles occasioned by his sister-in-law's remarks.

"Oh, dear!" exclaimed Mrs. Burton, "is there any more?"

"Only this. It's positively the last 'and finally.' We, then, that are strong, ought to bear the infirmities of the weak, and not to please ourselves. Again I would remark that I believe you're orthodox."

The Burtons looked very sober for a moment, when suddenly there came through the air the cry: "Pa-*pa!*" Tom sprang to his feet, Helen looked anxious, and the Burtons smiled quietly at each other. The cry was repeated, and louder, and as Tom opened the door a little figure in white appeared.

"Papa, I can't get to sleep," remarked Budge, shielding his eyes a moment from the light. "I ain't seen you for so long that I'ze got to sit in your lap till some sleep 'll come to me."

"Come to auntie, Budge," said Mrs Burton. "Poor papa is real tired—you can't imagine the terrible work he's been at for an hour."

"Papa says it rests him to rest me," said Budge, clasping his father tightly.

The Burtons looked on with considerable quiet amusement, until there arose another cry in the hall of: "Pa-*pa!* pa-*pa!*"

Again Tom hurried to the door, this time with Budge clinging tightly around his neck, and as the door opened, Toddie crept in on his hands and knees, exclaiming:

"The old bed wazh all empty, only 'cept for me, an' I kwawled down the stepsh, 'cauzh I didn't want to be lonesome no more, an' I'ze all empty, too, an' I wantsh somefin' to eat."

Helen went to the dining-room closet and brought in a piece of light cake.

"There goes all *my* good instructions," groaned Mrs. Burton. "To think of the industry with which I've always labored to teach those children that it's injurious to eat between meals, and worse yet, to eat cake!"

"And to think of how you always ended by letting the children have their own way?" added Mr. Burton.

"Eating between meals is the least of two evils," said Mr. Burton, "when a small boy is kept in bed with a sprained ankle and on a short allowance of food. Oh, dear! I see my subject nozing around again, Alice. Do you know that most of the wickedness of children come from lack of proper attention to their physical condition?"

"Save me! Pity me!" exclaimed Mrs. Burton. "I'm convinced already that I don't know a single thing about children, and I'll know still less if I take another lesson to-day."

"Izh *you* takin' lessons, Aunt Alish?" asked Toddie, who had caught a fragment of the conversation. "What book is you lynin' from?"

"A primer," replied Mrs. Burton, "the very smallest, most insignificant of A—B—C books."

"Why, can't you read!" asked Budge.

"Oh, yes," sighed Mrs. Burton; "but whether there be knowledge, it shall vanish away."

"But love never faileth," responded Mrs. Lawrence.

"If you want to learn anything," said Budge, "just you ask my papa. He'll make you know all about it, no matter how awful stupid you are."

"Many thanks for the advice—and the insinuation," said Mrs. Burton. "I feel as if the latter were particularly pertinent, from the daze my head is in. I never before imagined how necessary it was to be nobody in order to be somebody."

The boys took possession of their father, one upon each knee, and Tom rocked with them, and chatted in a low tone to them and hummed a tune, and finally broke into a song, and, as it happened to be one of the variety known as "roaring," his brother-in-law joined him, and the air recalled old friends and old associations, and both voices grew louder, and the ladies caught the air and increased its volume with their own voices, when suddenly a very shrill, thin voice was heard above their heads, and Mrs. Lawrence exclaimed:

"Sh—h—h! The baby is awake!"

The subsequent sounds indicated beyond doubt that Mrs. Lawrence was correct in her supposition, and she started instinctively for the upper floor, but found herself arrested by her husband's arm and anxious face, while Mrs. Burton exclaimed: "Oh! bring it down here—*please* do!"

The nurse was summoned, and soon appeared with a wee bundle of flannel, linen, and pink face and fingers.

"Give her to me," exclaimed Mrs. Burton, rising to take the baby, but the baby exclaimed "ah," and its mother snatched it. Then the baby did its best to hide in its mother's bosom. And its mother did her best to help it. And by the merest chance a rosy little foot escaped from its covering, seeing which Mrs. Burton hurriedly moved her chair and covered the foot with both her hands, though it would have been equally convenient and far less laborious to have tucked the foot back among its habitual wrappings. Then the boys had to be moved nearer the baby, so that they could touch it, and try to persuade it to coo, and Harry Burton found himself sitting so far from everyone else that he drew his chair closer to the group just to be sociable, and the Lawrences grew gradually to look very happy while the Burtons grew more and more solemn. And at last the hand of Mr. and Mrs. Burton met under the superabundant wraps of the baby, and then their eyes met, and the lady's eyes were full of tears and the husband's full of tenderness, and Budge, who had taken in the whole scene, broke the silence remarking :

"Why, Aunt Alice, what are you crying for?"

Then everyone looked up and looked awkward until Mrs. Lawrence leaned over the baby and kissed her sister-in-law, noting which the two men rose abruptly although Tom Lawrence found occasion to indulge in the ceremony of taking Harry Burton by the hand. Then the baby yielded to her aunt's solicitations, and changed her resting-place for a few moments, and the gentlemen were informed that if they wanted to smoke they would have to do it in the dining-room, for Mrs. Lawrence was not yet able to bear it. Then the gentlemen adjourned and stared at each other as awkwardly over their cigars as if they had never met before, and the ladies chatted as confidentially as if they were twin sisters that had never been separated, and the boys were carried back to bed, one by each gentleman, and they were re-kissed good-night, and their father and uncle were departing, when Toddie remarked :

"Papa, mamma hazhn't gived our sister-baby to Aunt Alish to keep, hazh she?"

"No, old chap," said Tom.

"I don't want *any* body to have that sister-baby but us," said Budge, "but if any body *had* to, Aunt Alice would be the person; do you know, I believe she was prayin' to it, she looked so funny?"

The gentlemen winked at each other, and again Tom Lawrence took the hand of his brother-in-law. Several months later, however, the apprehensions of the boys were quieted by the appearance of a little visitor at the Burtons, who acted as if she had come to stay, and who in the course of years cured Mrs. Burton of every assumption of the ability of relatives to manage *Other People's Children.*

THE END.

Lightning Source UK Ltd.
Milton Keynes UK
UKOW030250130312

188834UK00001B/4/A

9 781110 048120